T0243430

Advance Praise for *Funky*

"This is a wonderful and revealing look at one of the greatest American athletes of the last twenty years. From wrestling to MMA, very few have enjoyed success quite like Ben Askren has. The best part? He did it his way. Unapologetically. Even when most have advised against it. I have immense respect for the approach he took to life and fighting, and that comes through in these pages. This book is honest, and I'd expect nothing less from Ben Askren."

—Ariel Helwani

FUNKY

MY DEFIANT PATH THROUGH THE WILD WORLD OF COMBAT SPORTS

BEN ASKREN

PERMUTED
PRESS

A PERMUTED PRESS BOOK
ISBN: 978-1-63758-299-2
ISBN (eBook): 978-1-63758-300-5

Funky:
My Defiant Path Through the Wild World of Combat Sports

Cover Art by Rebecca Mindenhall
Interior Design by Yoni Limor

This is a work of nonfiction. All people, locations, events, and situation are portrayed to the best of the author's memory.

PERMUTED
PRESS

Permuted Press, LLC
New York • Nashville
permutedpress.com

Published in the United States of America
1 2 3 4 5 6 7 8 9 10

This book is dedicated to the many people who helped shape my journey. I surely wouldn't have gotten as far as I did without you. It's also dedicated to all of the kids out there who might be wondering if you have what it takes to make it. It's a long journey. You are going to have ups and downs and you may never reach the summit—but, when you look back in the end, I promise you, you'll never regret all of the effort you put in.

TABLE OF CONTENTS

FOREWORD

Changing a culture is not easy, but it was beginning to happen in our wrestling program at the University of Missouri. What we needed to get to the next level was a game changer—the recruit that would make that giant leap to become our first NCAA Champion. Who would that be?

In my early phone calls with Ben, his personality jumped out at me. Many people viewed Ben as arrogant or cocky, and maybe even a partier with his tie-dye shirts and the crazy stunts he'd pull at tournaments. Through our conversations, though, I really got to know him—and what stood out was his intelligence, as well as a passion for the sport that was not typical. Both his mindset and the belief he had in himself were extraordinary, and I loved it. Growing up as a coach's son, my dad would mention that the great ones possess a confidence that is rare, and it elevates the people around them to believe in themselves and makes others better.

Ben was his own person and I sold him on a vision to be the first NCAA Champion at Mizzou. I told him what coaches were saying about Mizzou—that we couldn't have a champ, that we couldn't compete in the Big 12, and that you couldn't have success in the international style if you went to Mizzou. I told Ben that was going to change, and he was going to be a big part of it. Ben liked being the underdog—the guy people doubted could accomplish things at a high level. He's also a big Muhammad Ali fan, which was something I learned along the way. I ended all personal notes to him with a quote from Ali. I'm fortunate to say my approach worked. Ben made the decision to come to Mizzou and the rest is history—or *Funky*!

I thoroughly enjoyed reading *Funky* because Ben is—and always was—so honest about where he was as an athlete. He never made excuses or blamed others. He always had a plan for what he needed to do to get better. He was willing to work tirelessly to get to that next level. Too many times we see the success that people have and think it was easy to obtain. Thankfully, Ben takes you on a journey through his entire career—how he developed physically, which was not easy, and how he developed mentally. He is the most advanced athlete I've ever coached on the mental side. *Funky* details the why and how he evolved into his funky style of wrestling. He shares the setbacks he incurred throughout his career and how he wouldn't let those deter him, but instead, let them drive him to figure it out, grow, and improve. His "beginner mindset" from the start of his wrestling career, through his MMA success, to his current passion of running the Askren Wrestling Academy, is a big factor—if not the biggest—of why he's had enormous success every step of the way.

Reading *Funky* reminded me of the importance of *why* I coach and how Ben positively impacted me for the better. It reminded me of the positive impact he had on his teammates, and now the young boys and girls he coaches at the Askren Wrestling Academy. The success he and his brother and all of the AWA coaches are having is not a surprise to me, and won't be to anyone who reads *Funky*.

Lastly, I called him honest, but he wasn't completely honest in the book...I did make the call to him before the Junior Nationals.

Brian Smith
Head Wrestling Coach
University of Missouri

CHAPTER ONE:
THE TRADE

"If you have the opportunity to play this game of life you need to appreciate every moment. A lot of people don't appreciate the moment until it passes."

—Kanye West

F irst of all, there was always the caveat.

When I retired from mixed martial arts (MMA) in late 2017, I actually meant it. I wasn't playing a game. I was thirty-three years old, undefeated, and a reigning champion, but I was fresh out of real challenges at ONE Championship, the Singapore-based promotion I was fighting with. Before MMA I was a two-time national champion at the University of Missouri, twice winning the Hodge Trophy as the country's best collegiate wrestler. Under the circumstances, walking away felt like the right thing to do. It was something I could control. What I had not been able to control was realizing a long-held desire to compete against the very best welterweights in the world, most of whom belonged to the Ultimate Fighting Championship (UFC). For a decade the UFC had been, for me, an exclusive club with velvet ropes, and my name—in spite of my accomplishments, and for reasons that remain mysterious to this day—was just never on the guest list.

So I retired after defeating Shinya Aoki in Singapore, but I added a caveat: I would remain retired, *unless I get the opportunity to prove I'm the best.* That left the door very publicly open for somebody to come along and change my mind. I emphasized this during a popular two-hour appearance on Joe Rogan's podcast in early 2018, one of the most watched pods Rogan did that year, making my position crystal clear.

Was I subtweeting the UFC by appending my retirement like that? Of course I was. But it was a justified subtweet. UFC president Dana White had planted the seed years before that I wasn't interested in fighting the best guys in the world, which meant plenty of fans in his echo chamber held this notion to be true. Whenever my name was brought up to him—which was frequently—Dana made it part of a running narrative that I was ducking real challenges and taking the easy path by fighting no-names in other promotions.

That claim couldn't have been further from the truth.

Anybody who knew me, going back well before I wrestled at Mizzou or competed with the 2008 US Olympic team, understood just what kind of competitor I was. I am obsessively competitive and always have been. You can't be the best unless you beat the best, and honestly, to me that meant the perceived best having *to beat me.* I'd been playing out fights with longtime UFC welterweight Georges St-Pierre in my head for years. I contemplated on an endless loop just what a great foil I would make for then-champion Johny Hendricks, a rival whom I actively disliked since wrestling against him in high school. Who doesn't love a heated backstory? Besides, I could do what no other welterweight could do—*I could make a Johny Hendricks fight interesting.* I thought about some of the welterweights I had ragdolled in training sessions during my early years in MMA—back when

I was just starting out in 2008-09—who were being coro-
nated on a weekly basis by the MMA media. I had it in me
to smash up a lot of old notions and ruin all of tomorrow's
parties, and I wasn't afraid to talk about it.

I knew damn well what I was capable of, but the problem
was I knew that *they knew*, too.

The other problem was, well, Dana simply didn't like me,
and public demand to get me into the UFC only served to make
him more stubborn about it.

So when I retired from fighting, I made sure to leave his
version of the truth in check on the chessboard for everybody
to compare notes against. It was an open challenge: bring me
on, or I'll call it a career. In truth, I was fairly content to leave the
competition of the fight game if it came down to it, and I could
do so with my head held high. I'd won titles in every promotion
I'd fought in and had compiled a perfect 18-0 record in MMA.
The only blemish was a bullshit "no contest" against an opponent who faked an eye injury out in the Philippines. In the year
2017, I was never hit once—not cleanly, at least—in three fights.
My accomplishments spoke for themselves.

But it was more than just that. I've always felt like athletes,
particularly in combat sports, hang on too long. I didn't want
to do that. I love coaching, and I was ready to give 100 percent
of myself to my students at the Askren Wrestling Academy
(AWA), the wrestling schools my brother Max and I run in our
home state of Wisconsin.

By the early fall of 2018, I was pretty far removed from
any thoughts of ever stepping into a cage again, which was
evident in my physique. As a person who likes to eat *way* too
much, I was filling out. I wasn't monitoring anything, and I
hadn't touched the surface of a scale in nine months. When
I weighed myself in September, I came in at a whopping 208
pounds, which is massive for a welterweight (170 pounds). I
was working out, doing yoga and other exercises, but I was
fat as shit. I wasn't doing any striking, any jiu-jitsu—really,

nothing in the way of actual fight training. I was just enjoying my meals for a change, something I hadn't been able to do without a pang of guilt for many, many years.

Still, even though the limbo stretched on, I always knew there was a possibility of something happening, that somehow—maybe through public demand, or in an epiphanic moment where Dana the businessman would come to the realization that I could make *him* money—I'd end up in the UFC. Accordingly, I continued to stoke those flames. You know, *just in case.*

To get my weight back under control during that plumping season, I decided to do an end-of-the-year wrestling tournament, the Midlands Championships, which is a big college tournament hosted by Northwestern University that's open for decorated wrestlers from the outside. I had the thought that, *Okay, I'll wrestle in this tournament just so I have to make weight for something, if for no other reason than to gain back a little discipline.* Going from 208 pounds to 174 would be a daunting task, but as a goal-oriented athlete, it made sense for my mental approach. It gave me something to center on.

It was a damn good thing I did. Fairly early on in my training for that, the CEO of ONE Championship, Chatri Sityodtong, got in touch and tossed out the word "trade" for the first time.

Trade? That word didn't even make sense. Trade *with whom*? And *for what*?

Chatri and I had maintained a great relationship from the moment I met him in 2012, back when my wife and I traveled to Singapore for a seminar for a sponsorship engagement with his company Evolve. That day, he saw me training with Rich Franklin, and he had an early idea of what I might be able to do if I came over to ONE. Throughout my seven fights under the ONE Championship banner, we kept in regular touch. He knew my situation as well as anybody. He understood that I still had the desire to prove I was the best in the world and it bothered me that I'd never had the opportunity to do so.

So, after I retired, I reiterated to him that I'd only come back if I had the opportunity to prove I was the best. He knew exactly what I meant. What that might actually look like, I had no idea. Was it going to be something of a co-promotion between ONE Championship and Bellator? Would they release me from the last couple of fights on my contract so I could go fight somewhere else if I had the chance and/or desire? Maybe they would sign a big name? There were a few scenarios in play, some of them just wild ideas, others semiplausible possibilities—all of them completely hypothetical. I knew he was genuinely trying to figure something out, because one idea would dovetail into the next. Maybe I could hop into that welterweight tournament Bellator was planning, a kind of poetic homecoming tour for me, the original king of tournaments? The name Rory MacDonald, the popular former UFC fighter who was fighting in Bellator, kept popping up, too.

Yet, as creative as I can be in my mind, a "trade" was something I'd never contemplated, not even as a passing flight of fancy. Why would it? To even *suggest* such a thing was foolish, if for no other reason than swapping assets in MMA just doesn't happen. Too many egos involved. Too much binding language in the contracts. Too many legal entanglements. Too much dissension in determining fighter value. It didn't help that the UFC was notoriously stingy with its roster, either. All contracts were constructed to work entirely in the UFC's favor, and they didn't have to bend where they didn't want to. Back in the day, when people were dying to see a heavyweight fight between M-1 Global's Fedor Emelianenko and the UFC's Brock Lesnar, Dana and Zuffa owner Lorenzo Fertitta flew out to Russia in an attempt to wrest the great heavyweight Fedor from his contractual bearings and sign with the UFC. To no avail. When Fedor made it clear it would have to be a co-promotion with M-1 Global, Dana treated the idea as preposterous. Even the *mention* of M-1 Global had him flushing red, as the UFC was light-years more accomplished.

Fedor, like me, was on Dana's shit list for a long, long time.

It was pretty obvious that Dana didn't much like competition, and he certainly wasn't looking to *work with* competition. He used to call Bjorn Rebney, my old boss at Bellator, "Bjork," and commonly referred to Strikeforce back in the day as Strike*farce*.[1] Whenever he mentioned Oscar De La Hoya—who promoted just one pathetic MMA card featuring a geriatric Chuck Liddell against a helium-headed Tito Ortiz—he blurted out the word "cocaine" like it was a Tourette's tic. As far as I knew, if he thought of ONE Championship at all he never really mentioned them. So to construct a trade with the UFC was too far-fetched to spend much time contemplating.

Yet....

Yet...here was Chatri, tossing out the word "trade" like we were in the NBA or MLB and about to switch cities. When he first mentioned it, I'd just moved into my new house outside Milwaukee, and he said, somewhat provocatively, "What if we trade you?"

I didn't know how to respond. I said, "What do you mean? I don't know what you're talking about—*is that even a thing*?" Then, before I'd even given it a second to sink in, I added, "Well, hell yes, if that's an actual real possibility, you can do whatever you want. I'm all for it."

The truth is, I didn't need to think about it. I'd been thinking about it for too long. It had been almost a decade since I'd had the opportunity to outwardly prove how good I was, and, even back then, the guys I fought were *close* to the best but not *the* best. When I fought Douglas Lima in Bellator, I think he was ranked in the sixth-to-eighth range in the pan-promotion welterweight class. When I fought Jay Hieron, he was around tenth or twelfth, and Andrey Koreshkov—whom I outstruck officially 248–3—was in the range of tenth to fifteenth. I'd never gotten to fight a legitimate

---

1   Of course, Zuffa later purchased Strikeforce and integrated the rosters.

top-five guy. I felt like I'd been disguised for a decade, and it annoyed me. I was ready. It took me maybe two seconds to agree on a Hail Mary "trade."

Chatri was like, "All right, cool, we'll look into it." He was very vague, which somehow made me think it was legit.

I swung back and forth between being doubtful and optimistic, but he'd piqued my imagination. It was an awesome feeling. When he got back to me again late one night, he conveyed that progress was being made and that he'd soon have news. What an adrenaline rush. I couldn't go to sleep that night thinking about it. I just lay there in a state of guarded excitement, thinking about the possibilities. Still, I wasn't completely sold. I'd been burned by the UFC before. Back in 2013, when I left Bellator as the reigning champion to test myself as a free agent, the UFC said they wanted me. I even went out to Vegas to meet with UFC brass and get a deal done. And then, just as suddenly, they didn't. They gave me the old bait-and-switch without explanation, and that's why I ended up with ONE Championship, "dodging," as Dana liked to say, the "real challenges."

This time felt different.

I kept overruling my doubts and thinking it was no longer a pipe dream, *this is real*, it might *really happen*. My chance to fight the best—*to prove I'm the best*—was on the cusp of finally coming through. A couple of weeks later, while attending my Mizzou teammate Mark Bader's wedding in Austin, Texas, I saw a message come through from Chatri stating that the trade was nearly complete. I'll never forget standing in line for food when I saw it. He said he was waiting on one more level of clearance, one last little hurdle to get over before I could be considered a UFC fighter. It was at that point that he revealed to me that I'd be traded straight up for the UFC's longtime flyweight champion, Demetrious Johnson, whom many—myself included—considered the GOAT in MMA.

Demetrious "Mighty Mouse" Johnson?

Talk about surreal. Johnson was the flyweight king who'd recently lost his title to my former teammate on the 2008 Olympic team, Henry Cejudo. He was never the draw the UFC wanted him to be, but he'd authored all the important chapters of the UFC's record books. He had more title defenses than Anderson Silva. He had more finishes than any flyweight in UFC history. He had the record for scoring ten-plus takedowns in three separate fights, which was a personal favorite of mine. That was a lot to part with to acquire a guy Dana didn't particularly care for.

Even if the UFC never learned how to market Johnson properly—and even if the UFC was so disenchanted by his curiously hard-to-market title reign that it was in the process of shuttering the flyweight division altogether—the optics were that they were shipping off a great champion. Demetrious as the trade bait made more and more sense as I thought about it. Johnson's longtime coach and friend at AMC Pankration, Matt Hume, was the senior vice president at ONE Championship, meaning they could be reunited in Asia. Demetrious was always chirping about his pay (or lack thereof) in the media, which didn't do him any favors with the UFC. At some point, what should have been a mutually celebrated dynasty turned into an acrimonious, faltering relationship. He was a burden the UFC no longer wanted to deal with. So he was sent packing, and a new burden was being welcomed in.

That new burden was me. And the new burden was *thrilled*.

What mattered was that the partition was coming down between me and all those glorified welterweights on the UFC's roster. For a guy who never likes to be wrong, this was an admission that Dana saw the value in bringing me aboard—a very public admission. It was a win-win for everybody involved, except maybe for Dana directly, who had been so openly opposed to me fighting for him for so long. In fact, if there was common thread between Demetrious and me as we crossed flight paths over the Pacific, it was that we could both say "Fuck yeah, Dana" and "Fuck you, Dana" and mean it either way. If he really believed that "when Ambien can't sleep, it takes Ben Askren," as he famously tweeted in 2012 when I was the dominant Bellator champion, he was about to get a super-heavy dose.

That alone gave the air in the fight world a charge. And I knew immediately that I would make my first UFC fight about more than me versus Fighter X. I would make it equally about the feud people had grown to love: me versus Dana. I would prove my worth to the UFC by poking the bear himself, and thus make us both some money.

Only…I had to wait to say anything. I was told I was to sit on the news until the paperwork was finalized and the UFC could make it official, which was going to take a bit. I am not a patient person, so not being able to put it out there was excruciating. Here I am, knowing this thing that I've waited so long for is about to go down, but I can't say a word. I was rendered powerless to control my own news. I don't like things being out of my control. Most fighters don't, which is why they prefer one-on-one competition to team-oriented sports where blame can be evenly distributed. As my wife, Amy, can well attest, my impatience can be extremely annoying to be around.

And in the age of constant interaction and social media, do you know how hard it is for an already impatient person to see people talking the same shit about you, or discussing fight hypotheticals they believe can never happen, when you know all that's about to change? It's murder. Holding a revelation for a period is a tremendous burden. As a week of waiting became two weeks, and then two weeks became a month, I was bursting at the seams to let everyone know. It wasn't until late October, shortly before Halloween, that I got word that the paperwork had been finalized, and the trade became official. I noticed right away that those three little letters—U F C—carried some serious import. Though I was the same guy who tweeted about disc golf and cryptocurrency and Mike Cernovich—niche shit that I was into and knew annoyed a lot of people—I experienced a sudden surge in popularity pretty much overnight.

The Tuesday it was announced I went to my oldest daughter's school to do my usual book reading to her first-grade class. In the half hour or so I read to the kids I'd gained more than five thousand new followers on Twitter. I had friends sending me screenshots of the notification they received of the news on the ESPN app, and my phone was blowing up. It was a crazy day. I'd always been active on Twitter, but suddenly people were flocking to my feed. Why? Because of the *UFC*. I guess the trade had validated me as somebody worth following, as if during all the preceding years I was nothing more than another league nonentity. That whole week, everybody in the combat space was talking about the trade.

To make it all official I traveled to New York that weekend, where the UFC 230 pay-per-view was about to take place at Madison Square Garden featuring a heavyweight title fight between Derrick Lewis and my former Olympic teammate Daniel Cormier.

Long before I landed in New York I could see that the trade was almost universally applauded. Demetrious was getting the fuck out of the UFC, where he would be able to start over/ flourish in a new (and perhaps more appreciative) market, and I was coming at long last to the UFC. There was vindication in the air, and not just for me, but for all the diehard fans who had seen me butting heads with Dana over the years.[2] The guy who called Dana a liar for proclaiming that the UFC couldn't drug test its entire roster[3]—thus incurring his eternal wrath—had stayed the course. In the soap-opera sense, the news was right in MMA's wheelhouse for juicy drama. Everybody knows Dana's vendettas are active obstacles and very difficult to overcome. In the end, somehow, I had overcome them, and now Dana would have to do something he never dreamed of having to do: promote a Ben Askren fight. This made me a sentimental figure in MMA circles.

---

2   It should be noted that I don't harbor any animosity for Dana. As I write my own story, I can reiterate what I've always known about myself: I don't hold any long-term grudges.

3   Shortly before Zuffa brought in USADA to regularly drug test its entire roster.

More importantly to me, the trade exposed a long-festering fib: I was never reluctant to go to the UFC. I wanted to be in the UFC going back to when I was a free agent in 2013, but I was just never given the chance. I'd only ended up at ONE Championship because that offer from Zuffa never materialized. I arrived the same smart-ass I'd always been, the same in-your-face wrestler, the same "Curly-Headed Fuck," as the British fans would soon call me. I was now free to double-leg all the celebrated worshippables at 170 pounds, and that thought was not only exhilarating, but shared. A lot of UFC welterweights couldn't stand me. And, given that I'm a smack-talking wrestler, many of them wanted nothing to do with facing me.

The news dominated the weekend in New York and overshadowed the pay-per-view a little bit. I did a media scrum that Saturday at the event and answered all the questions that could never be asked before. Namely: Who did I want to face in my first fight? The answer to that was pretty simple: Darren Till. He was the British fighter coming off a one-sided title fight loss against my friend and former Mizzou teammate Tyron Woodley, but he had plenty of juice to steal. He was open to social media volleys back and forth. He'd play along with me to build a big fight. Not only that, I knew I could take him down at will and do as I pleased, which would both piss a lot of people off and set me up nicely for an even bigger fight.

The media ate it up. Who doesn't love fresh blood in an already-stacked division, especially a party-crashing champion who can back up the talk? I arrived ready to talk. I had lived for the moment I'd be able to. It was fun to find myself the center of attention at an actual UFC event.

It was a perfect situation for everyone.

Except, it wasn't *totally* perfect. At least not for me.

It wasn't something I wanted to talk about—and realistically, it wasn't something people wanted to hear about—but I had a lingering hip issue stemming back to my college wrestling days that was getting worse by the day. At first I thought I was just getting old, which I was. But it wasn't that. Shortly after the UFC pulled the trigger on the trade for me and I started training in earnest again, the hip became an immediate issue. Up until that point I hadn't been training super hard, but when I cranked things up I knew it wasn't good. I found myself facing the reality that I might have—at most—a year to a year and a half before it got to the point I'd no longer be able to compete at a high level.

About a month after I'd come out of retirement, in December 2018, I went to see my doctors back in Columbia, Missouri, and told them it was bad, hoping there might a microscopic procedure they could do, something minor that could temporarily fix things up. They took some X-rays, gave me some PRP (plasma) shots, and then told me pretty matter-of-factly, "Yeah, it's pretty jacked up." They gave me the green light to go ahead and do what I was going to do for as long as I could take the pain, but they made it clear—and an MRI would later confirm—that hip replacement surgery was in my not-so-distant future. There would be no easy scope, and there was no way to tweak a few things to extend my shelf life. I had severe loss of cartilage, labral tears, and bone spurs to contend with, which meant my new opportunity would come with a shot clock.

And that clock was loudly ticking down in my ear.

With that, I knew I had to strike hard and fast in the UFC, because I wouldn't be afforded the luxury of a slow build. The year 2019 had to be my year. There is an old cliché in sports that you should never look past an opponent, because doing that looks (and feels) like you're taking something for granted (and therefore inviting disaster). What bullshit. Muhammad Ali wouldn't have ended up synonymous with greatness if he conformed to such tripe. Conor McGregor wouldn't have ended up on *Forbes*'s annual big earners' list if he wore blinders and focused on the guy in front of him and nothing else. Jake Paul would never have become the boxing interloper he's become if he wasn't out there planting seeds. In prizefighting, the big picture is the only view to take. You should have a bigger plan in mind at all times and execute it in stages—like a crumb trail to where you want to end up.

You think it just popped into Nate Diaz's head to call out McGregor after he beat Michael Johnson in Orlando, when he cut one of the best promos in UFC history? Hell no. When Nate ever-so-elegantly said, "Conor McGregor, you've taken everything I've worked for, motherfucker. You know what's the real fight, what's the real money fight? It's me," in his live-airing postfight interview with Joe Rogan on Fox, that idea was floating around in his mind long before he traded the first punch with Johnson. Johnson was the hurdle for those words, and those words were worth millions of dollars.

A smart fighter is always thinking three steps ahead.

Given my circumstances, I was already putting together a three-step plan for 2019, with an option for a fourth. I'd debut in March, hopefully against Till, then I'd fight at the UFC's big International Fight Week in July, then I'd fight at Madison Square Garden in November for the welterweight title. Once I had made history by winning my third title in my third promotion, I'd leave myself one last legacy fight. That would either come against the quasi-retired Georges St-Pierre, to try and topple the king of kings in the welterweight division, or I'd face the unbeaten Khabib Nurmagomedov, the lightweight GOAT who takes people down and pummels them on the ground just like me.

In either case, it would be big. And in either case, if all went to plan, I would leave the game after that fight, win or lose.

The bone spurs in my hip were arguing with this plan the whole time, however. I was limited in my range of motion, making it next to impossible to do the necessary training to be a world-class mixed martial artist. I couldn't get my knee over my chest to condense myself, something I'd been doing forever in wrestling. I couldn't get myself into the positions I needed to be in, and my balance was off because I couldn't shift in my usual instinctive ways. I had to learn to adapt and fight to my body's new set of rules, and even then the pain in my hip and back was chronicling, ever so loudly, my every move.

When I was in Singapore training for a ONE Championship fight, my Thai trainers kept wanting me to do these repetitions of strikes and kicks. They didn't speak English, and I kept trying to tell them I could only do certain things, that I couldn't kick with my left leg. I eventually had to have Chatri communicate to them that I couldn't do all they were asking. It was something I'd been working around as privately as possible but, in situations like that, was forced to openly concede.

Still, I believed I could overcome my hip issues, at least for another year, and I wasn't interested in asterisks. I wasn't going to whine and bitch about my hip.[4] After reading so many books on sports psychology, I was well aware of what excuses sounded like, in whatever order they're presented. I knew better than to make excuses in advance of a fight, or in review. I knew that when you try too hard to sway public sentiment on anything, critics will only dig in further. They will see a whiner, and never see anything other than a whiner. I also knew that first impressions can last forever. There were those fans who still saw the same clumsy striker from the early days beating Dan Hornbuckle to win Bellator's welterweight tournament in the guy facing Robbie Lawler in his UFC debut a decade later. I could live with that.

And I could live with some pain and limitations, too, as it didn't deter my goals. I wanted to win the UFC title to complete my collection of titles. Even with my limitations, I believed I had it in me to do that. My goal was to become the only fighter in MMA history to win titles in Bellator, ONE Championship, and the UFC—the three biggest promotions of my day. It was also to agitate as many UFC welterweights as I could, to whip the whole class into a frenzy.

Everybody knew that I'd never fight my friend and team-mate Woodley, even though when I came into the fold he

---

4   I know what you're thinking—*but you're bitching and whining now.* Hey, it's my book, where else am I supposed to tell you the facts?

was the UFC's welterweight champion. But guys like Kamaru Usman? Free game. I was the one who introduced him to the world as "Marty," as he was known back when he wrestled at Nebraska-Kearney. Guys like Colby Covington? I went at him mercilessly. Guys like Till and Masvidal? Easy pickin's. I had trained with Masvidal years earlier at American Top Team in Florida, and let's just say that our workouts weren't competitive (and Jorge knew it). I used everything at my disposal to get under the skin of everyone within earshot of the top ten. I could torment at will, and I was doing just that.

Oh, how they fumed.

I loved it. Especially when they found out how much the UFC was going to pay me. I hadn't had any direct conversations with the UFC up until the night before the deal was *done* done, when I spoke to the UFC's executive vice president and chief business officer, Hunter Campbell. It was weird. They had to create a new contract for me, because when they traded for my ONE Championship contract I only had three months left. That meant if the UFC didn't create a new contract and give me a fight within three months, they'd be screwed. We had to renegotiate right off the bat, and quickly. My manager, DeWayne Zinkin, took care of the money part and sorted out the numbers. For my first fight in the UFC I'd earn $200,000 to show and an additional $150,000 to win. Compared to other professional sports, that might not seem like a lot of money. But in fighting? In the UFC? There were guys who'd been competing in the UFC for years who weren't making close to that kind of money. There was plenty of resentment about that, for anybody comparing purses. And I soaked it up. I let all the old criticisms about being boring, schlubby, or afraid of legit top-five fighters instantaneously transform into criticisms about being overpaid and overvalued and over-arrogant. As long as they were talking, all was good.

I continued to push for a Darren Till fight right away. He was No. 2 at the time on the UFC's rankings and popular. I loved the matchup for me, especially as the maiden voyage to my three-step plan, but the UFC was pushing for a fight with the fading former welterweight champion Robbie Lawler. I didn't love that idea, because he had gone 1–1 since he lost the title to Tyron back in 2016. His lone win in that stretch came against Donald Cerrone, who had bounced up from lightweight to challenge Robbie. Then he lost a listless decision to another lightweight, Rafael dos Anjos.

I didn't see Robbie as the best option, but the UFC *really* wanted him. I was never told exactly why, but a lot of people think it was because Dana wanted to stick me in a bad stylistic matchup right away, to prove in my first big moment of UFC-sized scrutiny that I wasn't all I was cracked up to be. At a remove, I can admit I kind of agreed. Though Robbie had declined since his title run, he was definitely one of the tougher matchups for me out of all the possibilities. Till would have been a cakewalk. Lawler would take some doing. He had solid wrestling, he could get back up when down, and he could hit like a truck. Or at least, he could hit like a truck earlier in his career.

I agreed to the fight, because ultimately it didn't matter to me. The fight was scheduled for UFC 235 on March 2, 2019, in Las Vegas. As the narratives came into focus and people zeroed in on how I'd look in my debut, I just enjoyed myself to the fullest extent. The UFC PR people loved me right away. I never turned down interviews. I showed up to things on time. I no-sold the shark-eyed Lawler in ways that made everyone believe I was playing with fire. It was brilliant. How could I be so calm when about to step in there with a killer?

Outside the brewing hoopla of the trade and everything that came out of it, I went back to training as the same guy I'd always been since I first got serious on the wrestling mats as a kid. I wanted to fight in the UFC, but psychologically it was no different than the thousands of wrestling matches I'd had growing up. I like to paraphrase the old Rudyard Kipling poem:

If you can dream, and not make dreams your master, and think while not making thoughts your aim...when you come to meet with triumph and disaster, you treat those impostors just the same.

There was really nothing to be tense about. I learned that pretty early on.

CHAPTER TWO:
THE BEGINNING

"There are only two mistakes one can make along the road to truth; not going all the way, and not starting."

–Buddha

As specific as my memory can be, my recollections of how I began wrestling are a little hazy. One of my true passions in life is disc golf. If you were to ask me how I did at the United States Disc Golf Championship in 2011, I can zoom into the most granular details, especially on the last hole when, down by one, I tried to bomb an anhyzer to tie the leader and ended up sailing it a little right and into the woods. I bogeyed and lost by two, finishing in second place. That's easy, but I'm like that on random days on the disc golf course, too. I can play seventy-two baskets on a given day and tell you exactly what happened on every single one, even sometimes if the day in question was a year ago. My mind is a reliable replay machine when it comes to the things I'm really into.

Yet, if you ask me when the great love of my life began—when I started getting into wrestling—it's like trying to recall a dream. There are scattered memories, little flashes of the old wrestling room at Arrowhead High School in the early days when I was on the kids' club, recollections of my younger brother Max and me wrestling all over the house, but when did it all actually begin?

I believe I was in first grade when I joined the kids' wrestling club. I only remember that I didn't really like it because I wasn't very good at it. I was a rambunctious kid, but it didn't hook me initially. I played different sports from a young age, and it was baseball that became my first true love. The Oakland A's were my favorite team. It was 1990, and the A's had that loaded lineup with Jose Canseco and Mark McGwire. I loved the long ball, and the "Bash Brothers" were jacking home runs left and right. You watched what was on television and listened to what was on the radio, and back then that was America's pastime. As I developed into a decent enough third baseman, my allegiance shifted to the local team in Milwaukee, and I became a diehard Brewers fan by mid-elementary school. I can remember Robin Yount recording his three thousandth major league hit and really feeling the magnitude of the feat.

Baseball had a lot of charms for me, both as a fan and a player, but I have no real memory of watching wrestling early on, even in person. The first time I can remember going to a meet was in fifth grade, when I attended the high school state tournament. It was a dark sport, for the most part. Obviously there wasn't any streaming going on, and no highlight packages on *SportsCenter*; unless you were scouring for it in trade magazines, coverage of the local wrestling circuit was minimal.

After my first season I wasn't super excited about wrestling, so my dad got some of my friends involved to rekindle my enthusiasm. He had brought home some wrestling mats to roll around on, a couple pairs of boxing gloves, and some other roughhousing equipment for Max and me. Max was two years younger than me, so he took the brunt of the beatings, but that wasn't what concerned my dad. He was tired of us taking over every room in the house, so he made the downstairs into a kind of restricted area for rowdiness.

For whatever reason, wrestling crept up on me slowly. As I look back as an adult, it's funny—I'm naturally combative and very physical, so it feels like something I should've been into right away. But I wasn't, and I'm fascinated (not to mention slightly baffled) that the kid version of me was so slow to catch on. Though I was essentially a fat kid with very few kids my own size to compete against, I began liking it a little better the second time through. By the fourth grade, I was getting pretty decent at it. The meaning of wrestling began to make sense to me. There was something about the one-on-one competition that felt tailor-made for me, even if my kid brain couldn't explain it or fully understand why.

I have two vivid memories from my childhood sports teams that led me (somewhat indirectly) to the mats. The first was with the local youth soccer team in the third grade. It was late October, and we were having typical Wisconsin weather for that time of year—rainy, shitty, cold. I wasn't an all-star soccer player by any means, but I desperately wanted to win and was out there giving it my all, elements be damned. I wanted everyone else to want it as badly as I did, yet my team was being a bunch of sissies. They couldn't get into it. Because it was cold and wet and miserable, they just wanted to go home, and that attitude was reflected in their play. It infuriated me. I was distressed that nobody else would give an effort, and it bothered me that it was so thoroughly out of my control.

Two years later, while playing with the Lake Country Chiefs football team in the fifth grade, I had a similar experience. We had a relatively good football team, but the team we were playing, the Sussex Sabercats, was way better than us. Everybody knew it, and it pissed me off how easily it was accepted as a foregone conclusion that we'd lose the game. Once Sussex got up by a bunch of points, my teammates wanted to just end it and go home. The huddle turned into a bunch of whining. I was like, "Screw this, I came to play football!" I remember being deeply annoyed that I'd be forced to share in a loss with people who were giving up. I didn't want that to be a reflection of me or, more to the point, what was inside of me.

I wasn't giving up.

If these weren't pivotal moments, they were at least small epiphanies for a kid figuring out his own psychological makeup. In team sports I had a say in things but lacked total control over the outcome. Looking back, that idea is one of the key reasons wrestling appealed to me more and more. In wrestling, you can control your own destiny, for better or worse. It's you out there on an island, and it's your account-ability alone that stands trial. *Whether I fail or succeed, I control the switchboard.* I liked that idea early on because, for lack of a better way of explaining it, I was the only one I knew who could reliably match my own intensity. If I was going to fail at something, it had to belong to me alone. I had to be in sole possession of the outcome.

So, by the spring of fifth grade, I understood this about myself, or at least had a solid inkling. I quit baseball that year to devote more time to the one-on-one sport of wrestling from April through June. By then I felt comfortable rolling around, having wrestled with my brother Max on the mats my dad got us.

People have asked me whether my dad might've had ulterior motives in bringing those wrestling mats home. Did he sense something in Max and me from those early times, believing he could steer us toward wrestling? That would've required some serious foresight. My dad is a blue-collar Midwestern guy who has made a career in submersible pumps. He dabbled in sports during his own childhood—track and field, football, even wrestling a little bit—so he understood a boy's need to romp around, but the answer is no, probably not. Honestly, I think he was mostly just looking out for our furniture. I broke things like it was my job as a kid (and still do to this day). He provided us a place to go throw each other around, we used it, and we inadver-tently began to love it.

I'd say it was sometime around that same fifth-grade year that something crystalized for me. I began taking wrestling seriously, if somewhat unconsciously at first. Thoughts of wrestling techniques began to take over my daydreams of other sports. In short, I began to give myself over to it. As I mentioned, I was a chubby kid in fifth grade, weighing around 130 pounds. I was having a little success, but I didn't have many kids my size to wrestle. That meant the whatever weight brackets I found myself in at tournaments were sparsely populated.

My parents were always supportive of my athletic pursuits, and wrestling was no different. There weren't many tournaments at that age—and at that point in time in America's Heartland—but they made sure to get me to what few there were. One of the early ones I competed in was the Northern Plains Regionals, a seven-state tournament held in Omaha. I took second place, mostly because there were a grand total of three kids in my bracket. It was bittersweet to come in second in a three-man race. On the one hand, I could truthfully say I came in second, and that would sound pretty cool without the burden of context. On the other hand, I knew. I knew I wasn't better than, say, twenty kids from the region, like you'd find in the far-more-filled-out lighter weight brackets. I was just one of the best out of a small handful in the big-boy bracket. Who the hell wants to celebrate perfect mediocrity?

Here's where my memory begins to lock into the details a bit more, where it begins to feel like wrestling was a major part of my life. As a big kid I was picked on quite a bit in school. I wanted it to stop, and I had this desperate urge to get better at wrestling at the same time, so I decided to take a drastic measure. At just eleven years old, I decided to lose a bunch of weight so that I could compete with the kids in the lower weight classes. Without any pressure or prompting from my peers, my parents, or my coach, I dropped thirty pounds in sixth grade. I went from 130 pounds to 100 pounds, which, for me, was like reinventing myself.

Thirty pounds.

That's some serious discipline for a kid still two years shy of meeting the PG-13 movie rating. It was a pretty prescient move on my part. It's the first instance that I can pinpoint where I did something like that, where I took a direct action toward meeting a goal. I was getting plenty of exercise with wrestling and other activities, but I recognized that I needed to monitor my diet. I had the wherewithal to tell my parents to buy specific groceries to help me out. It was at that precise moment that I stopped eating desserts. I was in Wisconsin, "the Dairy State," yet I quit eating pizza at a time when most kids were apeshit for pizza. It was tough. I stopped drinking soda and eating any kind of fast food, a resolve that became part of my permanent scaffolding; to this day I don't drink soda or eat any kind of fast food. It was in those little omissions that I whittled down to my new one-hundred-pound frame. My parents let me do my thing, and I did it. By enforcing my decision, I learned something about my own power of will. I proved something to myself.

That felt good on many levels. For starters, kids no longer singled me out because of my weight. It was something I now had control over. At a hundred pounds I was right in the wheelhouse weight of the best competition, and I could find out what I was really made of.

At first it didn't pay off. With all the kids competing at that weight, I wasn't having as much success as I used to. I lost my share of matches. But by the seventh grade, as I dedicated myself more and more to the sport, things began to change. I won my first Youth State title that year at UW Stevens Point, which was a big deal for me because I'd worked so hard for that. It was the first time I'd achieved a higher level of success, where I won something kind of big. The next year, as an eighth grader, I repeated the feat—I won the Youth State title again.

Now wrestling wasn't just a sport to me. It was in my blood. Yet none of my sports heroes were wrestlers.

Not that I worshipped any athlete growing up, but the sports figures I admired most were fairly different from one another and spoke to me in different ways. Given that he was a towering figure of my Wisconsin youth, I was a big fan of Green Bay's own Brett Favre. I was a huge Packers fan all the way through middle school, and watching Favre play was an almost ritualist appointment. I had a deep fondness for the late Steve Prefontaine, the long-distance runner who competed in the 1972 Olympics. I had several books about him, and I think some of that might've had a bit to do with my mom. She had been a walk-on for the Iowa State gymnastics team, and she was very consistent. She once ran for a thousand days in a row, three miles every day, just because it was what she wanted to do. I think there was a correlation there to Prefontaine when I was young. I became a big fan of Lance Armstrong, too, the cyclist who won the Tour de France seven times in a row. (Confession: even though most see him as a disgraced athlete, I still like him.)

The athlete I looked up to the most, though, was Muhammad Ali, who fought his last fight in the boxing ring some three years before I was even born. I was drawn to his outspokenness and audacity as much as I was to his ability to back up his words. I could understand from a pretty young age that he stood for more than just being a famous boxer, that he fit the contours of greatness through a boldness of spirit. Mostly, I loved that he was this larger-than-life figure who understood sports psychology better than anyone. He told you exactly what he was going to do and then did it. He won people over with his bombast as well as his conviction, and then would go out there and exceed the wildest expectations. To me, he was fascinating. I had maybe twenty books about Ali, and I learned something about his competitiveness in each of them. I found myself wanting a rival like he had with Joe Frazier, and I wanted to be doubted as he was with George Foreman in the "Rumble in the Jungle." I wanted to know what it was like to not only be in a big moment, but also to conquer that moment.

I recognized the pageantry of it all, too. For whatever reason, I never got that much into pro wrestling, though I have to admit there was something about the showmanship and the theatrics that always spoke to me. As a moderate fan, I would watch the shows from time to time with my friends, *Monday Night Raw* mostly, the occasional Wrestlemania after the fact. Like many real wrestlers of the 1990s, the more I got into amateur wrestling, the more defiant I was about the fictitious realm of pro wrestling. Real wrestlers would push back on the fake stuff. It was insulting to compare the two, though—if you think about it—both come from the same place if you go far enough back. I can remember defending the sport from the spectacle, and being astonished at people's gullibility to believe that the soap opera on TV was real.[5]

I was more into the literal realm of taking people down and pinning them. By my freshman year in high school, I decided to make it my last year of doing anything other than wrestling. I had gotten pretty decent at football by then. I was a 119-pound nose tackle who could leverage my weight enough to push a center back, and I loved tackling people. I just felt ready to give everything I had to wrestling, so ninth grade was the last year I'd put on the cleats. Wrestling was it for me. I wrestled as often as I could.

Unfortunately for poor Max, that meant he became my original throw dummy. I kind of big-brothered Max that year when I couldn't find a training partner. He learned to push back the best he could, but I toughened him up whether or not he was ready for it. I can remember saying to him, "Hey, Max, I need you to wrestle me." He'd always be like, "no!" So I'd give him a kind of ultimatum: "All right, I'm going to fight you or you're going to wrestle me, one of the two." Sometimes he'd say, "Go ahead, beat me up." Other times he'd think better of it and decide to wrestle. He was in the sixth grade. He didn't start enjoying wrestling until a little bit later on, maybe around his freshman or sophomore year in high school, but he was in deep when I'd come calling. He had his head on the swivel, and he was always on the lookout for my takedowns.

---

5   Nowadays the amateur wrestling world could actually take notes from fake wrestling.

That year I made the high school state finals, which was a roller coaster of emotion. I got there but lost in overtime to a kid named Joe Henning from Chippewa Falls, 9–7, which was really discouraging. I can recall every detail to this day. I got down 7–2 and cradled him and just about pinned him to tie it 7–7. Boom, I had all the momentum. I felt great. I had him gassed!

But then, ugh—I blew it. He beat me 9–7.

Still, I was finding more success in everything I was doing in the freestyle and Greco-Roman spring stuff.[6] I was practicing more than anybody I knew and honestly believed that I was practicing more than anybody I didn't know. With no year-round wrestling clubs for other kids to participate in, I saw it as an advantage. I just kept plugging along every single day on my own, forcing myself to train. I wrestled and wrestled, and believed I was working harder than anybody else within a thousand-mile radius—more than anybody anywhere. I was obsessed.

A big turning point for me was when I went to the one and only national tournament for kids in the fifteen-to-eighteen-year-old range in Fargo, North Dakota, representing the state of Wisconsin.[7] It was a tournament I had been thinking about for years, and I'd had my guns trained on it for a long time. This would be my first time stacking myself up against a who's who of kids my age from all over the country. I was amped to get in there and showcase myself and let all the work I'd put in pay off. I knew this would be my moment to arrive.

Wrong. Wrong, wrong, wrong.

I went 0–2, scoring a goose egg in the biggest tournament of my life! It was a huge letdown. We drove five hundred miles just so I could flop in both matches, which was a serious blow to me. I had gone all-in on wrestling. I believed in my abilities so thoroughly that I'd never considered the idea of losing. To

---

6   Freestyle and Greco are the Olympic styles of wrestling; if you compete in the spring and summer, it is most likely a freestyle or Greco competition. Freestyle is much like folkstyle with a slightly varied scoring system, while Greco is limited to the upper body, so it comes with a lot more high-amplitude throws.

7   These days there are a ton more opportunities for wrestlers at that age, but that's what I had. That's what I had!

come up that short? It wasn't even a reality check; it was a reality rewrite. I remember I kept saying to myself, "Damn, am I really this bad?" I fell in love with wrestling because it was up to me to fail or succeed. It turned out that losing stuck around a little longer. It also turned out that the sting of losing was disproportionate to the thrill of winning. You savor a win for as long as you need to. You dwell on losses forever.

I can't say it was a humbling experience, exactly. It was depressing is what it was. The recurring idea that you're not as good as you think, with the overruling (and unwelcome) idea that you're not good at all, well...it was a lot to process. At that point in time there wasn't any place to get a quick measure of redemption and put it behind me. It was mid-July, and there weren't a lot of tournaments. It would be months before I could wrestle again in high school. I was forced to live with it one way or another, and much of that time was spent interchangeably between states of depression and resolve. I thought I had made a gigantic amount of progress, and I thought I was getting to the point where I'd make some waves nationally, yet I wasn't even close.

Buzz.

Kill.

Still, something happened at the nationals in Fargo that year that would change the way I approached competition forever. My coach on Team Wisconsin, Terry Steiner, gave me a talk after that poor showing about what he perceived to be performance anxiety. It wasn't something I knew much about, and I certainly didn't know I had it until I had it. But he seemed to identify immediately what would come to eat at me for the next few months, which was actually very simple: I hadn't performed my optimal best, because I was overcome by the moment.

He told me that I had made the big match different—that I gave it additional gravity. As I reflected on it, I knew he was right. I got there and I thought, *Oh my god, this is Fargo, the national tournament; I've been hearing about this for years! If you win here you usually get a college scholarship.* I'd been reading these wrestling magazines, and you get to looking around and you see the kids who are ranked and mentioned in there. You think, *Oh my gosh, here I am among these guys— that guy's a state champ, and that guy's a state champ.* You're in brackets with a hundred people, far bigger than anything you've experienced before, and your eyes get big. There are all these possibilities and all these heightened thoughts, and frankly, well...what I came to realize is, when thinking it over, it's all bullshit.

Coach Steiner pounded home that point specifically, and it was a game changer for me. I had all that stuff swimming around in my head, and it was completely irrelevant. Yeah, the kids were pretty good. So what? Should I have gotten killed by them? Hell no. I was so busy marveling at who was in the tournament and the magnitude of the event and all the exposure it could give me that I performed like shit. I blew things out of proportion, and the consequence of that was an early exit.

I vowed not to let that happen again. I got back at it in the weeks after the tournament, this time in pursuit of the even keel. I kept grinding and began consciously downplaying big moments in my head, blocking any mental obstacles as I envisioned the setups. The idea I worked on was what Coach Steiner told me—one match is no different from the next, and one tournament no different than the other. Treat everything the same.

That lesson stayed with me as I entered my sophomore year at Arrowhead, and it paid off.

Though I was still largely shy and withdrawn socially entering the year, I really came into myself, not only as a wrestler but as a person and—truth be told—as an antagonist. That winter I discovered online high school message board forums and was immediately drawn to them. There was something about the anonymous interaction that pulled me in, specifically when I was at the center of the conversation.

Wrestling consisted of the regionals, the sectionals, and the state tournament. I would spend a lot of time before these reading adults literally spew vitriol about me. It was fascinating. I returned fire on there often and soon discovered that I enjoyed stirring the pot. This was a development. The idea that you can work people so easily was something I was fascinated by, and, though it was still years away from becoming an identifier on social media, I was drawn to the art of trolling.

Part of the hate I was receiving came down to my style and how I carried myself on the mats. I'd set some personal goals before the season that I was hell-bent on realizing. In fact, I was hell-bent on smashing them. The all-time high school record for takedowns in Wisconsin was set at a fairly respectable 235. I shattered the record by scoring 371. All I did was take people down and let them up, take them down and let them up, over and over and over. I was highly skilled and found myself going against kids with a much lower skill level, and I was essentially just torturing them. When I wasn't doing that I liked to carry around a boom box.[8]

As expected, it pissed people off, and they wanted me to know just how much.

I remember somebody alerting me at the sectionals tournament that there were all these people talking shit about me on the forum. I had lost badly to a kid named Spencer Dominguez[9] as a freshman, and we developed a rivalry when I won the rematch fairly decisively in a dual meet earlier in the year. There was another kid at the same time, a senior named Trevor Spencer, who attended Baraboo and was undefeated. That gave people all the ammunition they needed. All over the forums people were saying that *this* Spencer would beat me or *that* Spencer would beat me.

I was doomed by the Spencers!

I ate it up. I remember thinking, without getting all that emotional, *Fuck these people—I'm going to kill these guys.* I would tell these people with their silly pseudonyms as much

---

8   Or, as we called it back then, a "ghetto blaster."
9   I actually coached his nephew years later.

online, but I understood it wouldn't mean anything until I went out and did it. I knew I carried the ultimate trump card: it was me in there that had final say, as I was the one competing. It was an extension of my control to lead the peanut gallery—in this case, full-grown adults—to their disappointments.

I ended up beating the first Spencer—Dominguez—in this crazy match in the state quarters, 12–11. Then I faced the other Spencer—Trevor—in the state finals, and I straight-up tortured him. I won 21–8 to win the state title at 130 pounds, the exact same weight I'd been as a sixth grader. I couldn't be denied. Performance anxiety? Not this time. I was already well into sports psychology, and this time I had my mindset dialed in the right way.

That was me coming into my own. I'd come up big in a big event. I didn't just compete well, I killed off any residual traces of self-sabotage, and that's what gave me the biggest sense of accomplishment. I was crisp, clean, and ready to compete. After I beat Trevor Spencer, I did what I'd been dying to do—I went on the forums and taunted everybody. It was one of the sweetest victory laps ever.

With the success of having won a state title, I began dreaming a little bigger. I'd long wanted to wrestle collegiately, but after my sophomore year, I somehow convinced my parents to send me to the Olympic Trials in Dallas...by myself. This was in the year 2000, and USA Wrestling was running a camp alongside the open trials, and I felt I had to be there. Within reason, my parents were generally hands-off. They kind of let me do my thing without too much meddling, but this was a big ask. I remember how thrilled I was when they gave it the green light.

It was a leap of faith to do that, as it was the first time I'd ever done anything on my own. I had never flown on an airplane by myself or stayed in a hotel room by myself. This was an adventure. I was saddled with a roommate in Dallas, but we weren't all that monitored by adults, and—to my surprise—there weren't any chaperones. I don't recall bed checks or anything like that, so I could have done whatever I wanted.[10]

But all I wanted to do was immerse myself in the wrestling scene. I went to the camp and loved every minute of it. I went to that tournament and absorbed it like I had nothing before in my life. It's funny, but, at that point, I'd never watched an NCAA tournament or championship. I'd never watched the Big Ten, and in fact, I'd never even seen a Division I dual meet. I had never seen such a high level of wrestling in person, and catching my first big glimpse affected me tremendously. I can remember feeling the energy of the guys making that Olympic team and how that ignited my passion. I wanted to experience that someday, too.

It was at that moment—out in Dallas, Texas, at just fifteen years old and without any real supervision—that I set my goal of becoming an Olympian. It wasn't a pipe dream to me, because I believed so much in my resolve. Even if I wasn't as talented as other kids or gifted with perfect genes and athleticism—which I was absolutely not[11]—I had a counter. I could outwork anybody. I *would* outwork anybody. I could push myself harder than anyone for as long as it took. I had this drive in me to put in the work until it hurt and then tap into my resolve and put in more work. This showed up in the meets, as I could wear opponents down and break them in the end. From that moment on, the Olympics became the goal. Doing the math, I thought I'd be too young for the 2004 Olympics in Athens, so I'd aim for the 2008 Summer Games. Watching that tournament in Dallas made me realize just how badly I wanted to do it. I'd never had a goal become such an obsession so quickly.

My plan went like this: make the Olympic trials in 2004 and then make the Olympic team in 2008. Easy, right? Hell no, it

---

10   I feel certain I was the only idiot at that age who didn't take advantage. Then again, I guess that's why my parents had a lot of faith in me. They knew I was serious about my pursuit and had confidence I wouldn't do any stupid shit.
11   I hadn't even all-American'd yet.

was the hardest thing imaginable—but I recognized how hard it would be and used that as a frame of reference for how hard I'd have to work.

Later that summer I went back to Fargo and placed fifth in Greco and went 5-2 in freestyle. I had performed far better than the first time through, but—against the best young talent in the nation—I still came up a little short. It was disappointing, but this time I didn't need a psychological reboot to understand why. I was hindered by a nagging neck issue that affected me that whole summer. At some point during competition in my sophomore year of high school I kinked my neck in a match. I didn't think anything of it and wrestled through it, but as time went on it became more and more painful. In Fargo it was a little more debilitating than it had been, which prompted my mom to set up a doctor's appointment and then a session with a physical therapist when I got back to Milwaukee. Not really expecting anything terrible, I was blown away with what the doctor told me.

He looked at me gravely and said that I had the same injury that Green Bay tight end Mark Chmura had, which was a terrifying comparison. Chmura had a herniation between the C5 and C6 discs in his spine, and—with the increased risk of paralysis now a factor—his football career was cut short because of it. The doctor told me that if I continued to wrestle I could become paralyzed, too, and therefore I shouldn't wrestle anymore. Those words landed with a thud.

Not wrestle? Hold up...*paralyzed*? Me? The kid who has just learned to harness his will to trump other kids' wills while pinning them on the mat? I was shocked he was saying this. I looked at him and remember thinking, *That's the stupidest thing I've ever heard.* I didn't say out loud what I knew right then and there—I wasn't going to stop wrestling.

Now, I have a tendency to trivialize things like injuries and illnesses, especially when it feels as though somebody is over-reacting. I don't see things as all that serious unless I know they are. I never do. I had my finger snapped into an odd angle wrestling in Belarus years later and just kind of looked at it as if a lie were being told to me by my hand. My daughter, Alex, had a respiratory virus at six weeks old and had to go to the hospital for two days, which I guess makes it pretty serious, but the whole time I was like, whatever. She can't blow her nose so she needs some snot sucked out, so what? I can't help it! It's just not my way to overreact.

As alarming as it was to hear a doctor tell me I shouldn't wrestle anymore, especially at such a young age, I never took it seriously for one second. Maybe it was defiance or that I thought myself invincible as a teenager, but that assessment struck me as not only overcautious but truly absurd. My parents didn't seem all that worried about it. My mom forced me to see a physical therapist, but my dad— an old-school blue-collar type—just told me to tough it out. My high school coach, John Mesenbrink, wasn't overly concerned about it, either. He told me to "get it stronger and let's go get another state title next year." It hindered me late in my sophomore year, but I ignored the doctor's cautions and kept wrestling, with my only compromise being that I'd stop doing the Greco-Roman style that involves more throwing. As I went along through my junior year I barely noticed it, to the point that that doctor's visit felt like a strange, particularly arbitrary dream.

I repeated as a state champion.

I wrestled better than ever before. In fact, I wrestled as much as I possibly could. My parents used to take us on ski trips to Colorado, and that year, right after wrestling season, I didn't want to go. When it became clear that I had to, I found a two-day tournament going on in Denver that just happened to coincide with our visit dates. I asked my parents to leave me in Denver while they skied in the mountains. Once again, they trusted me enough to do that. They left me for the day and got back in time to watch me in the finals.

The same summer I decided to grow my hair out. Up until then I kept it close to shaved, so I had no idea that my actual hair was curly. It was kind of a shock to see just how curly. I looked like a young Apollo as it grew out, and it was quite a spectacle. By the time wrestling season approached, my hair had grown fairly long, which couldn't help but rub some people the wrong way. I think it was because I looked a little rebellious, like I was trolling the idea of an all-American wrestler (or my better-shorn counterparts). Some people saw it as arrogance, and others saw a punk-ass kid with a curly Afro rubbing it in everybody's face. Whatever they saw, I know one thing: I liked that it pissed people off. And I loved taunting them.

To make that easier, I created my own forum just to antagonize them as much as I could. Before a big tournament, I'd log on and not only bask in the hate I'd encounter there, but actively egg it on. They'd rag on me about everything—my hair, the way I dressed, the boom box, my body, whatever they could find to band together on. I didn't realize it at the time, but it was a turning point for me in how I saw the world, and how I thought about things in general. It was a firsthand lesson in understanding how group psychology works, how it mounts, how it moves, and, ultimately, how it can be manipulated. I came to this realization a full decade before social media apps like Twitter were even a thing. It was something I took with me to the University of Missouri and to every platform I visited in MMA. When dealing with haters is inevitable, make dealing with haters fun. I would stick a virtual tongue out at them, and it bothered them even more that they couldn't get to me.

Yet things were being said beyond just the forums my junior year.

My parents always allowed me to find my own way, yet they were tuned in enough to see what was going on. Occasionally some of the stuff being said about me would get to them far more than it got to me. At one point that year my mom sat me down and showed me a wrestling video, which struck me as curious—what the hell was this about? Then she drew me a picture of my hair—a big exaggerated Afro, disproportionate to any human face—to try and illustrate just how stupid she thought it looked. It was her way of trying to convince me to cut it. Didn't work. I was like, "Mom, that's stupid—it's my hair, I'm not going to freaking cut it. I don't give a crap what these people say."

The thing was, throughout its history wrestling had always been highly regimented, extremely rigid in how it conducted itself and very protective of its identity, and I think people saw the long hair as a sign of disrespect. To tradition. To the sport as a whole. People saw me as a rabble-rouser, which, for the most part, wasn't entirely untrue. I did like ruffling feathers. Yet I was about a lot more than that. I loved wrestling. I was fortunate that Coach Mesenbrink allowed me freedom of expression to do the things I wanted to do and to be myself. Mesenbrink gave me leeway and let me become my own individual, yet he did that because he saw how hard I worked in practice. I was the hardest-working kid in the gym. I was all the way in. He knew it, and everybody who knew me knew it.

That year I defeated a kid named Dustin Hillman in the state finals, 20–5. It was a great feeling to win again, but I wasn't all the way happy. I wasn't all that interested in state results. I had lost perhaps the biggest non-title match of my career against the No. 1 wrestler in the country that year, Marcus Levesseur, during the Bi-State in-season tournament. I didn't just lose; I got my butt kicked. I wanted that match bad, and losing it drove me to work even harder than I had before. Still, as summer approached, I had a date circled.

On July 1, when colleges were free to recruit the best high school wrestlers in the country, I got exactly zero calls. Total silence. Nothing. Coach Mesenbrink, who always went above and beyond for me, actually made some tapes to send off to colleges to help drum up interest. Yet, without a ton of national success and with a little notoriety as a troublemaker, I felt like there was a bit of a stigma on my name.

I knew that one of the reasons for that was that the University of Wisconsin's coach, Barry Davis, had perpetuated the notions that I was anti-authority and that I didn't work hard. All of it was bullshit, but that was the word.[12] My outward demeanor might have suggested rebelliousness, but I didn't drink, I didn't smoke, and I never had. In fact, the truth was I wasn't rebellious at all. Davis had made a value judgment on me without taking the time to get to know me. I might've been a little anti-authority, sure, but I wasn't anti-wrestling. I had vowed to myself to outwork everybody. And I would outwork his efforts to hinder me, too.

With the recruitment spurn still stinging, I went back to Fargo and, at long last, had a breakthrough at the national level. I beat the No. 1 kid in the country, Troy Letters,[13] and took fourth place, losing to the future two-time Oklahoma State national champion—and eventual UFC welterweight champion—Johny Hendricks. That turned the tide for the colleges that were on the fence with me. The phone began to ring. I heard from Edinboro, Wisconsin, Arizona State, and Northern Iowa. I also heard from Brian Smith, the head coach of Missouri. I took my first unofficial visit to Columbia in August before my senior year and fell in love with it.

My senior year at Arrowhead was once again dominant, and I was bumping up in weight classes in an effort to find challenges. At this point my skill level was far beyond any challenges in Wisconsin, yet during the sectionals, while competing at 171 pounds against the No. 2 guy in the state, Luke Griffiths from West Allis Central, I injured my ankle on the first takedown attempt. He ended up taking me down three times before I got on top and pinned him. I won the match, but my ankle was really jacked up. I went to the hospital and learned it wasn't broken, but I couldn't put any weight on it. Still, I went ahead and hobbled into the state tournament, and—somehow—found a way to win the first match. Problem was, I couldn't stand up.

---

12   Well, mostly bullshit. I still have a problem with authority.
13   He went onto win an NCAA title at Lehigh and become the head coach at Clarion.

I lost my second match, and that was that. There would be no state title for me as a senior.

I went through five weeks of rehab to get my ankle right, but it felt like an eternity. I had circled an event in which I'd make my return. Wisconsin was hosting something called the Dream Team Classic. It's lost some of its bigness over the years, but back then *Wrestling USA Magazine* would put together the best team from the US, and states would bid on it when they had a really great class of kids. Wisconsin was flooded with talent that year, so it was held there. I had wrestled Hendricks the previous summer in Fargo and he had killed me, so he was the gauge to see how far I'd come. He was the No. 1 guy in the country, and generally unbearable to be around.[14] My rematch with him at the Dream Team ended up being 7–5, much closer than the first time, yet I was still on the short end.

Later that summer I returned to Fargo for a fourth time, and this time I won it at 171 pounds. I beat Jake Herbert, who ended up being an NCAA champion, and whom I'd be facing a few more times in college. It was the first time I'd won something big on the national level, and it was the perfect ending to a wild ride that saw me go from the wrestling mats my dad brought home to winning a national tournament that I'd busted my ass for.

Now it was time to see where it was all leading. The first stop: Columbia, Missouri.

---

14   He only got more unbearable as he went into MMA, and it's painful that we never got to fight there, you know what I mean?

CHAPTER THREE:
FINDING THE FUNK IN COLUMBIA

"Nothing is given to man on earth—struggle is built into the natural of life, and conflict is possible. The hero is the man who lets no obstacle prevent him from pursuing the values he has chosen."

–Andrew Bernstein

Coach Brian Smith will tell you that he called me before that big Fargo tournament between my junior and senior years, when all the very best high school wrestlers in the country were being recruited and I was feeling completely shut out. All these years later he maintains that he did, but...let's just say we have differing memories on that. I distinctly recall feeling a sense of rejection before that summer's tournament, and I was using that as fuel going in. I was pissed off that the phone wasn't ringing.

In any case, when Coach Smith did call me (to my recollection) right after I took fourth that year in the tournament,[15] I was instantly intrigued. The University of Missouri was not a wrestling powerhouse, but they were a solid program, and they were the first to show real interest. That gave me a positive feeling from the start. Maybe all the first-tier wrestling factories with long, established programs had tuned me out, but Missouri hadn't. It meant something that Mizzou saw me for what I was and recognized the potential I could bring to the team. In my mind, they were the first college to truly see what the big programs were missing, and that sense of discovery matched up well with my motivation to make everyone who ignored me regret it. So I listened to Coach Smith when he called, and somehow, before I'd begun truly exploring my options, he talked me into coming on an early, unofficial visit that August before my senior year.

Looking back, I think he knew. I think he had a feeling I'd fall in love with Columbia and the program and the vision he had for it, and he wanted to give me a glimpse of it all before I got down to the business of official college visits. He knew that an upstart program might speak to a kid like me who fed off of the snubs and doubled down on his resolve each time he felt slighted. He knew some of the kids already in the program would sell it in ways that would speak to a seven-teen-year-old kid ready for his first big adventure.

I went down to Columbia with my mom just before high school started that August, mostly just to get a feel of the town, the people, and the situation. There's no way to accu-rately convey the impact that visit had on me, because it was such a youthful awakening at the time. I had a great time. From the moment I arrived I loved everything about Columbia, a quintessential college town tucked away like a secret halfway between Kansas City and St. Louis. It was all by itself out in the middle of nowhere, with trees and a river and a bustling campus. Having grown up about an hour

---

15   I beat the No. 1 kid in the country, Troy Letters, but ended up losing to Johny Hendricks of Oklahoma State.

from the University of Wisconsin, the idea of college life in Madison wouldn't have felt completely removed from home.

Columbia would.

Better yet, I immediately bonded with the guys I met on that initial visit, which did away with any foreign feelings a kid who'd never been away from home might have. Mark Bader, who hosted me that first trip, took me under wing right away and showed me around. Bader made me feel like I belonged from the moment we shook hands. I hung out a lot with team captain Jeremy Spates, an all-American who went on to become the head coach of Southern Illinois, and Kevin Herron, who would become head coach at Seckman High School in St. Louis. They were all way older than me; they'd all be seniors by the time I'd be a freshman. Right away, they felt like mentors, guys who had the knowledge I wanted and the experience I could use and learn from. The fall semester had started at Mizzou, and they took me to some block parties in the neighborhood. It was an amazing time. I felt right at home.

The bond I made with those three guys on the first visit was immediate and lasting, as all three remain good friends to this day. They were also pivotal in helping me decide on coming to Mizzou. They weren't just these fun guys with noses for good parties, they were also the foundation for Coach Smith's vision to put Missouri wrestling on the map, to bring the program up to a new standard and compete with the Minnesotas, Iowas, and Oklahoma States—all the dynasties of college wrestling. It mattered to them to get better, to keep the program moving full steam ahead.

I enjoyed myself so much that I couldn't stop thinking about the possibilities in Columbia upon returning to Wisconsin. During my senior year of high school I took my five official visits, which is what the NCAA allows athletic recruits. I visited Edinboro in Pennsylvania and the University of Northern Iowa in Cedar Falls, both respectable schools with good programs and pretty compelling pitches. The problem was they were small towns, *very* small towns, and I wasn't sure I wanted to spend the next five years of my life in either place. I visited Arizona State, which had a good tradition and a strong reputation, but it had an equally strong reputation as a party campus. I wasn't sold that the guys there were taking wrestling seriously enough.

The other school I visited was, of course, the University of Wisconsin.

Being from the Milwaukee suburb of Hartland, the University of Wisconsin in Madison was the school I was most familiar with. Actually, that's an understatement. I'd envisioned wrestling at Wisco from a fairly early age, and I became a big fan of Donny Pritzlaff, a two-time NCAA champion.[16] I wanted to represent Wisconsin on the collegiate level just as I had my whole life growing up. I really wanted to be a Badger, and I had assumed throughout high school that the Badgers would want me.

Wrong.

Of all the schools I visited, I was most annoyed with Wisconsin, especially when I found out that Badgers coach Barry Davis had been telling people behind the scenes that I wasn't very good. For a seventeen-year-old kid just coming into his own who'd never missed a single practice in high school, I took it personally. It felt like sabotage. Having interacted on the message boards, I knew pretty well that adults could act out in surprisingly petty ways, but I wasn't quite sure what I'd done to warrant such treatment in this case—especially from a coach with that kind of influence. Davis, for reasons I never fully understood, seemed intent on damaging my reputation before I even truly had a chance to build it.

The question I wanted him to answer was: *Why?* Did I have an arrogance about me? Sure. Did I have a smugness about my ability? No doubt about it. I wanted to be the best. Did I buck convention here and there and do things my way? Of course I did. It's a coach's job to see through to the person and to help bring out his greatest potential. My coach in high school, John

---

16   Whom I'd later beat, by the way.

Mesenbrink, allowed me to be me, which I needed to flourish in my own way. Davis didn't care for the high school me, and I guess he felt compelled to let it be known. The usual dynamic between a kid and an adult is that the adult is the one who gets to be disappointed in the kid's behavior.

That wasn't the case here. I was the one who walked away disappointed.

I wasn't a bad person, and I sure as hell wasn't a bad wrestler. Of the five schools I considered, Wisconsin was the only one that felt completely offensive to me, given that I was from the state, just an hour down the road. Wisconsin was in my blood, yet they didn't bother offering me much of a scholarship. That was a slap in my face, and I have to say it stung for just a minute. Still, I've always been super pragmatic (sometimes to a fault), and my more rational side kept inter-jecting on behalf of any college that was harvesting doubts about me. After all, I had underperformed in the national tournaments to that point, and I knew it. I hadn't made the impression that some of the other kids had, and I was sensi-tive to that, too. I understood—on some reluctant level—why schools might be skeptical.

So I packed it all into my resolve. Wisconsin didn't want me? Fine. I accepted it and focused my attention on the school that did. I went on my official visit to Missouri and essentially confirmed what I suspected all along; Columbia was the place for me.

I made my commitment in mid-November of my senior year. If I was a blue-chip prospect, that chip would sit mightily on my shoulders as I donned the black and gold. The truth was I knew how good I was, and I knew what was in me to do, so it really bothered me that the big colleges—Iowa, Minne-sota, Penn State, Oklahoma State—didn't recruit me at all. That stayed with me. I knew some of the kids who were heading to those schools, and they weren't better than me. Even if they were, they wouldn't be for long. I wasn't a gifted athlete, but I was driven and I was competitive. A competitor can do tremendous things with a perceived slight. Amazing things. Historic things. And Coach Smith tapped into that.

On my official visit he sold me on the wrestling program and the direction of the team. Mizzou was an up-and-coming program on the cusp of breaking through in a big way. He showed me that, above all else, the Tigers were devoted to winning. That in itself was enough, but what closed the deal for me was how Smith saw me fitting into that plan. He envisioned me as Mizzou's first national champion. The university had never had a national champion, and so he dangled a carrot out there for me to do something not only personal but historic—to be Mizzou's Trojan Horse on the national wrestling scene. The program was right there, and I was the one who could help get the Tigers over the hump. That got me fired up, as I truly believed—not just in my heart, but in my head, and in the core of my being—that I could be a collegiate national champion. These motivations were what I was working with. I couldn't express it to Coach Smith at the time, but I was hell-bent on making his vision come true.

Of course, it didn't take long for me to come crashing back down to earth. I was redshirted my first year, which I'd expected coming in, and that meant I couldn't wrestle in the main varsity events. I did get to compete in the open-tournament stuff, and there were some hard lessons to be found there, especially early on. That year, 2003, was rough and at times humiliating. I hadn't yet filled out physically, which was evident to everyone in the room, a room filled with absolute monsters who worked me over regularly. Future UFC champion Tyron Woodley was there at that time, competing at a weight class lower than mine but already a beast. So was the all-American Scott Barker. You had guys like Kenny Burleson and Jeremy Spates doing their thing, all-Americans who were lifting Mizzou into the national spotlight, squarely on their shoulders. I was learning from, and getting pounded on by, some of the very best in the country. It was a blessing and a curse.

Though I won some matches here and there in the open tournaments, I took a bunch of losses, too. It didn't just humble me; it left me searching for answers. I'd just achieved the pinnacle of success in high school. I felt invincible heading into college and believed myself ready to take the next step. Now, suddenly, I couldn't beat anybody.

Or so it felt.

I lost ten matches over a six-week period. Losing ten matches in such a short span was like being sucked into a black hole. I'd lost just eight total matches throughout my entire high school career; hell, I would go on to lose just eight matches the rest of my college career, but I didn't know that yet. I had hit an early crisis, and, to put it mildly, it was eye-opening. I realized that I wasn't close to where I wanted to be, and it bothered me in ways I could never have anticipated. That whole season I kept asking myself, is wrestling something I can even do at this level? Is this something I can and should keep pursuing? Is there something I need to change, or do I need to simply accept I'm not that good? All the doubts that come with shattered expectations and failure were flooding me each and every day that I was getting manhandled in practice.

Yet, just like when I'd come up short in that first national tournament in North Dakota, that redshirt year also served as a kind of turning point. I was taking losses because physically I wasn't in the same ballpark as these guys. When lifting in the weight room, or running "stadiums,"[17] or doing any of the workouts, I couldn't keep up. I wasn't nearly as strong or as quick as the high-end collegiate wrestler. Being an awkward kid with the Afro gave me distinction, but not any usable advantages. The losing in the tournaments only compounded all these spiraling developments, leaving me at a breaking point where I kept asking myself the same question, over and over and over: How in the hell do I break this funk?

---

17 Coach Smith would have us run up and down all the staircases at Memorial Stadium, where the football team played, which was a kind of existential hell.

As it turned out, by discovering it.

I remember telling ESPN a couple of years later in the NCAA national tournament that I developed my unorthodox style out of desperation.[18] That is completely true. I was desperate to compete. After interrogating myself and introducing so many doubts about whether I could succeed at the college level, I came around to my three basic options.

I knew I could dig in, meaning I could just keep doing the same things I'd been doing to get me this far, banking on the hope that—through sheer doggedness of will—things would turn around. I could innovate my style by taking traditional elements of wrestling and adding a spin, some kind of idiosyncrasy to enhance my strengths. Or I could pivot to something completely new. As a work in progress who loved and understood sports psychology relatively well, I was assessing myself by standing back and contemplating the best course of action as rationally as I could.

Of course, I knew what I had to do all along.

I would have to innovate my style. Late into my redshirt season and upon entering my freshman year of competition, I found the funk. What did that mean exactly? I was always conventional in high school, very good in the neutral position, using the take-'em-down-and-let-'em-up method to domi-nate matches. That wasn't working in college, so I'd inno-vate through scrambling. I'd un-inhibit my natural instinct to scramble. I started working with our volunteer assistant coach, Mike Eierman, who'd wrestled at the University of Nebraska and was instrumental in my evolution. Eierman was on the cutting edge in terms of innovation, and the emphasis he put on turning matches from literal physical dictations into some-thing a little more cerebral was tailor-made for me.

Scrambling at this point was very much looked down upon and thought of as junk wrestling, but the more I inves-

---

18 "Unorthodox" is a word that I heard a lot in college. It was the go-to word for people who had trouble understanding what it was they were watching. Un-orthodox. Kind of a funny word.

tigated positions, the more opportunities I realized people were leaving on the table. My ability to exploit these opportunities would become my calling card and help me transform the sport.

I understood I had decent length and could leverage the more prototypical wrestling build, which is generally muscular and squat. My idea was to add entirely new positions to hold opponents in a state of reaction and anticipation, meanwhile putting on a pace that would eventually break them. In other words, I'd use my two best assets—my brains and my motor—against superior athleticism and muscle. I'd make wrestling figure me out, rather than toiling to figure out how to neatly fit into the contours of tradition. This was a game changer for me, a newfound ability to rethink and reinvent. As my redshirt year went on, and I began winning more matches, I started to believe I could match up with anybody. It wouldn't matter if a Goliath got in my way; I'd make them dance to the out-of-tune music that I alone was making.

Innovating my style really was an act of desperation, but it was also zeroing in on a solution to regain control. If that meant modifying traditional approaches and aesthetics, so be it—the beautiful thing was that there was a method to the madness, and when people caught up to what it was they were watching, it was like the slow dawning of a revolution. Why shouldn't the improvisational aspects of a scramble become the real story of a wrestling match? It was all leading to the objective of pinning the guy in front of me. To my knowledge, the mad scrambling as an objective had never really been done before. People loved it. People hated it. People were confused and threatened by it. It looked high risk for conventional thinkers, and it was totally different for wrestling traditionalists. It wasn't artful, but it was relentless and—most importantly—it was *me*. It was who I was. It was everything inside of me working frantically to turn the tables in my favor, to run in colorful counter to the smooth-rolling norms.

In the simplest terms: I did what I had to do to adapt and, ultimately, conquer.

That redshirt year was perhaps the most important of my college days because it was the impetus for that scrambling, the method that would define me as I went on to rewrite the record books at Mizzou. After that year I qualified for the 2003 World Team trials, which was the highlight of the year because it gave me a real inkling that things were starting to come together.[19]

In my first official match of my college career, I went up against the guy who'd become my collegiate arch nemesis, Chris Pendleton of Oklahoma State. I got up 7–1 in the match by winning a pair of crazy scrambles, which demonstrated for the first time just how effective (and peculiar) the innovations to my game were. I ended up losing the match in overtime, 9–7, but it had been a promising start. Despite the loss, the bigger picture for the program was that Missouri had beat Oklahoma State for the first time in history. Before that, OSU was a dominant 24–0 against Mizzou. It was a seminal moment for the program, and one that Coach Smith would savor as we went forward. There was an anticipation in the air as to how far I could take things in the 174-pound division. It turned out pretty damn far.

I went 32–5 that freshman year and earned all-American honors, while also being named a finalist for the Schalles Award (given to the nation's best pinner). In the Big Twelve Championships in Ames, Iowa, I ended up going against Pendleton again, whom I'd lost to four times that season and who was cruising to a national title with a 28–0 record. With some familiarity between us, we had a very tough match, only this time I put him on his back with a scramble cradle, which brought the crowd to life. I won the match 9–7 in overtime to take home the championship and was named the Most Outstanding Wrestler at the tournament. It was not only an enormous upset, it was my first major collegiate breakthrough.

---

19   However, the results at 2003 WTT were embarrassing. I lost by fall to Pat Popolizio, who is now North Carolina State's head coach, and 6–0 to Randy Pugh, who is now an assistant at Northern Iowa.

I became the first freshman in Mizzou's history to reach the finals at the NCAAs, which were held just 125 miles down the road in St. Louis. As the sixth seed in the 174-pound bracket, I defeated Pennsylvania's Matt Herrington and faced Lehigh's Brad Dillon in the quarterfinal round of what ended up being one of the more memorable matches of my college career. We went back and forth in regulation, and he tied it late to force the one-minute overtime. With the Missouri crowd at the Savvis Center on my side, I won a ridiculous scramble, got a takedown and a three-point nearfall to win 12–7. For a lot of people, it was the first time they'd seen the update in my scrambling style on the mats, making opponents shuffle to the tunelessness of the funky beat.

Though I defeated Tyler Nixt of Iowa in the semis, I came up short against Chris Pendleton in the finals, 11-4. The Tigers were coming up; that much was certain. And the 174-pound weight division knew I had arrived. That year I began to fill out physically. I still had that goal of making the 2008 Olympic team, and everything I was doing was working well toward that goal.

On the international level I was making good progress, too. I did fairly well in the Olympic Team Trials in Indianapolis that year, taking fourth place overall despite being far too small for the 84kg class (185 pounds). I lost to Oklahoma State's Muhammed "King Mo" Lawal, whom I'd matched up against a year earlier in the university nationals and therefore had a little familiarity with. He was a hulk compared to me, wrestling collegiately at 197 pounds (to my 174), and that size difference played a major factor. I also came up short against the two-time all-American from Cornell, Clint Wattenberg.[20]

What meant more to me at those trials, though, was that I beat the world silver medalist and three-time all-American, Brandon Eggum in the consolation finals.[21] That was huge.

---

20 People know Wattenberg as an MMA guy now, as he's with the UFC's Performance Institute. They don't realize that at one time he was a great wrestler.
21 Eggum is now the head coach at the University of Minnesota.

I remember I was able to have some decent basic hand-fighting and defense against Eggum, preventing him from getting to any of the stuff he wanted to get to, and eventually I front-headlocked him to score three points. It was the biggest victory of my life.

By my sophomore year I was blossoming into what I'd projected myself to be when I signed on to wrestle at Mizzou, but I came up just short of becoming a national champion. Though I went 34–3, I found myself once again a runner-up for the 174-pound title, losing once again to my nemesis Pendleton in the finals after breezing through Oklahoma's E. K. Waldhaus and Illinois's Pete Friedl. It was disappointing. Pendleton just had my number.

One of the strangest stats of my college career was that seven of my eight overall losses came against Pendleton.[22] Though all the matches were relatively competitive, he was the bane of my existence during the first half of my college career, and the monkey wrench to my reaching truly historic heights in college. After all, if Chris Pendleton doesn't exist, I'm the second-greatest folkstyle wrestler of all time behind only the great Cael Sanderson.[23] Since Pendleton did exist, and he was in the same conference as I was and we found ourselves crossing paths at the same tournaments over and over, there was a force out there driving me every day to get better. For whatever reason, I just couldn't solve him. Over the course of his career he lost to guys that I would beat, yet math in combat sports is always misleading. The truth is, he was just tough as hell, and I respected him for that. I would lose a match to him, practice where I went wrong, and add a wrinkle for the next match, and he'd come in with a different game plan. Small evolutions. He kept me guessing, and—as rivals do—I like to think I kept him on his toes, too. I was always gunning for him.

---

22 The other was Purdue's Ryan Lange during my freshman year, who snuck one out on me 3–2.

23 Sanderson was 159–0 and remains the undisputed folkstyle king.

Halfway through my time in Columbia, I felt on the verge of something big. The team was on the cusp of becoming a big-time college wrestling program, which was a huge point of pride, and personally I knew I was ready to completely take over my weight class. I was also coming into my own as a person. I was an athlete who definitely had no problem speaking his mind, but I wasn't going to let regrets become part of my narrative, and I never wanted to be anyone's redemption story. What I wanted was to be as present as I could in the moment and to dominate, and my life on campus reflected that. The education mattered to me. In retrospect, I wish I'd studied business at Mizzou, but I was a geography major, and I was dutiful in maintaining a good grade point average.[24] I won four Academic All-Big Twelve honors. I liked to have fun, but I didn't drink, do drugs, or do anything other than work toward my goals of becoming a national champion and making that 2008 Olympic team.

In fact, the only time I willingly took anything throughout five years of college life was when I lost a bet with the heavyweight on the wrestling team, Kevin Herron. We were out playing at the Oakland Disc Golf Course, and he said he would get it closer to the pin than I would, an absurd proposition that I openly laughed at. He bet me, demanding I take a dip of tobacco if he won. Thinking he had no chance in hell, I immediately agreed, then proceeded to hit a tree with my throw. He did not hit a tree. I ended up taking the dip.[25]

I look back at the people I had around me before the start of my junior year and don't think I could've been surrounded by a better cast. I lived off-campus with my teammates Matt Pell, Amond Prater, and Mark Ellis, all of whom were as dialed in as I was. Coach Smith gave me

---

24 Hey, it was easy. Plus it would come in handy later when I was fighting in places like Grand Prairie, Texas, and Kallang in Singapore.

25 Disgusting. Of course, there was also the pot brownie incident, though that happened many years after college. Someone left it in the downstairs fridge by accident, and my mom thought it was a protein bar. She offered it to me, and I ate it and watched the walls melt for the next hour.

plenty of rope to do the things I wanted to do, as long as I worked hard in the gym. Like Coach Mesenbrink at Arrowhead High, he encouraged my style as well as my sense of self-expression. In fact, back when I began experimenting with the scrambling, it was Coach Smith who encouraged me to work with our volunteer assistant, Eierman. When he saw that it was working, he encouraged me to teach the other guys the techniques that Eierman had helped me with, because he was all about innovation.

And really, those other guys became the bedrock for my time at Mizzou. It was Bader, Spates, and Woodley who had provided something in my scaffolding that I knew was unshakable. Everyone was such a big part of everyone else's life. We essentially lived, ate, and fought together for five years straight and, in that time, became very close as not only a team, but as a movement with a shared purpose. I loved going to war with those guys. Tyron became a great friend and remains so to this day. Our lives traveled a succinct enough path where—years later when we were both champions in mixed martial arts—he was coming up to Roufusport in Milwaukee to train, spending as many as six weeks in town each time through. Other than his forays into the worlds of acting and rap music, our paths have run pretty parallel.

That whole team was special, including my good friend Matt Pell. We got recruited together out of Wisconsin and were roommates for three years during my time in Columbia. Pell was one of the marvels on the team. After moving up three weight classes, he ended up taking third his senior year and was a big reason Mizzou took third in the country. The younger guys coming in were also buying into what we'd been doing. Raymond Jordan and future Bellator champion Michael Chandler came in two years into my time at Mizzou, and they evolved into fantastic wrestlers. I took both under wing and did my best to mentor them. It mattered to me to be a good example to those guys as I entered what would be my biggest year to date.

If there's a storied part to my college career at Mizzou—the legendary run that people would revisit throughout the next decade as I ventured into MMA—it kicked off during my junior year. I was ranked No. 1 going in, which put a certain kind of pressure on me to deliver. I loved it. I was right at home amidst that pressure. I was already knocking on the door of breaking J. P. Reese's all-time pin record (set at forty-seven), and I knew I'd accomplish that fairly early on. I'd worked on my penetration and timing on my shots in the offseason and in summer tournaments, as well as my stance and motion techniques—things that I'd reviewed and pounded my head over after dropping that final match in 2005 to Pendleton. The one thing I felt certain about heading into my junior year was this: that Pendleton loss was soon to become a collector's item.

I was never going to lose again.

I was like a 174-pound demon of curls and cardio on a kill spree. I was apologizing to nobody, and never once was there a thought (or even a distant uneasy feeling) that I would lose all season. At the Cliff Keen Las Vegas Invitational I broke Mizzou's all-time pin record and then pinned Ohio State's Charlie Clark to raise my total to fifty. I would go out there and try to lock up a cradle or a hammerlock as tight as I could, then go for the pin as quickly as possible. I kept seeing and hearing the word "dominating" that season, as in "Ben Askren is the most dominating college wrestler in the country." It suited me, and, really, I led the chorus. I let people know! I set a school record that year with twenty-five pins, en route to my third go-round at the NCAA tournament in Oklahoma City. All-American? Get the hell out of here with that. I was on another level entirely. I plowed through Lehigh's Travis Frick (TF 19–3) and Hofstra's Mike Patrovich (TF 21–6) on my way to a third appearance in the NCAA Finals—this time against Northwestern's undefeated juggernaut, Jake Herbert.

Herbert was undefeated coming into the match and had taken out Iowa's highly touted Mark Perry in the semifinals to face me in the finals.[26] It aired on ESPN, and the eye test for the uninitiated was comical. Here was a yoked college specimen with muscles forming on top of his muscles, against a gangly, slightly hunching dude with a mashed-up face and an unruly Afro. The building was electric, and I felt invincible as I stepped on the mats. I was in a zone, at the perfect pitch for a competitor. After coming so close to tasting the ultimate glory in folkstyle wrestling the previous two years and working my ass off since the moment I stepped foot in Columbia, I knew it was my time. No psychological barriers could keep me back, no performance anxiety would creep in, and no living thing could keep me from realizing the promise I'd made to Coach Smith when I came in. It was a foregone conclusion that I was about to become a Division I national champion.

I didn't just beat Herbert; I freaking destroyed him.[27] I picked him apart, winning 14–2. Just like when I'd beat Trevor Spencer in the Wisconsin State Championships six years earlier, I felt like I'd let the rest of the world in on something I'd known all along, through every doubt and every practice and every setback and every run up and down the staircases at Faurot Field. I'd always known I had what it took to be a champion.

Now I literally was one. The endless private toils and hard work had paid off.

It was arguably the hardest route to a national title that year. Everyone knew I was good, but beating the undefeated Herbert, who would go up a weight class the next year and later win a pair of national titles and the Hodge Trophy (handed out to the year's best wrestler), left no doubt that I was the best college wrestler in the country, no matter the division. It capped off a year in which I went 45–0. I won the Schalles Award for

---

26 Perry was a beast. He went down to 165 pounds and won NCAA titles there over the next two seasons.

27 I know, I know—not exactly humble here. But there's so much humility in this chapter, this shit had to even out.

pins, and a few weeks after winning the national title took home the Hodge Trophy, which was the highest achievement of my life. As a kid who fell in love with wrestling in the fifth grade and had dreamed of the Hodge for years—college wrestling's freaking Heisman Trophy—it was surreal.

It meant just as much to me that Mizzou had its first ever national champion, just like Coach Smith and I had talked about when he recruited me. I'd met a goal, and there were some heavy doses of "I told you so" in meeting that goal, too. For all those big-time wrestling factories that hadn't recruited me, I couldn't have been happier to rub it in their faces.

After winning a national title, I also caught a nice glimpse of the other side to a fan's perspective. In high school, as a stubborn kid who defended himself on the forums and kept winning just to rub their noses in it, I endured quite a bit of antagonism. People didn't want to see me win back then, and my defiance on that point pissed them off. After winning the national title in college, a strange thing happened: I was almost universally liked, in large part because of the Cinderella element in play. I went to Mizzou, and Mizzou had never had a national champion, which made us the darlings of the dance. America loves underdogs. Storylines are always more meaningful from the unsung perspective of the David figure trying to overthrow a Goliath.[28] I was a breath of fresh air, and everyone was pulling for me and Mizzou to break through.

The "funky" style became a thing after that. With the visibility the event got through ESPN's national coverage, I did tons of interviews before, during, and after, all centered on the unorthodox approach I took to getting it done. I was the outspoken kid with the curly Afro, the hippie folkstyle wrestler who overcame the guy whose deltoids had multiple definitions (as nouns, verbs, and adjectives)—it was like nothing they'd seen before, and everybody wanted to know more about me. Better yet, I wasn't a machine like some of these

---

28 Even though I was the Goliath of college wrestling that year. Shh.

muscle-bound guys; I was more like a cog in the machinery. Years later, FloWrestling did a video feature on me highlighting people's bewilderment of that match with Herbert, while demonstrating the exotic elements I brought to it. Mimics surfaced almost immediately, and "unorthodox" was suddenly in fashion.

But, as always, wrestling has a way of pulling the rug out from under you. Between my junior and senior years a good deal of those triumphant feelings diminished through a series of unexpected setbacks. I wrestled in the US Open and—to my extreme disappointment—didn't end up placing. That was a crippling blow to whatever feelings of invincibility I'd built up over the last season. Competition is a cruel and ceaseless master. I was still a little undersized for the 84kg international weight, it was true, but I couldn't lean on that as an excuse. The main thing was to keep plowing ahead, especially with the World Team Trials coming up a month later.

In late April 2006, while training for those trials, I began to feel some discomfort in my neck—similar to what I had felt in high school when the doctor grimly advised me to quit wrestling. It was gradually getting worse by the day, and it was turning my regular training into daunting undertakings. One day I was doing some warm-up bench presses at 50 percent the weight that I'd normally do, and as I brought the bar down I couldn't budge it. My spotter helped lift it off me, and I told him to do it again. I brought it down and once again couldn't budge. I was like, *What the hell?* I had very little strength in my left arm.

All I wanted to do was put it all to the side and get through the World Trials, but after visiting a doctor I realized there wouldn't be any World Trials for me that summer. I'd be forced to take some time off, which ended up being a period of just over a month. With where I was in my wrestling career, that felt like five years. It was absolute torture. A young college champion who is ready to showcase on the world stage doesn't idle easily. He sits and stews and drowns himself in what-ifs. In the end, though, the rest period was probably the best thing for me heading into my senior year. I recovered my strength, and the neck issue—just like back in high school— kind of mysteriously faded away.

I was ready to make some history my senior year, and this time I'd do it with my brother, Max, right there with me. Max, who competed in the 197-pound division, was entering his freshman year at Mizzou as a highly touted prospect. By December we were both ranked No. 1 in the country, which was one of the rare times in NCAA history that a set of brothers topped the rankings simultaneously. Everything was firing on all cylinders, and the whole team was amazing that year.[29] I personally went on a kind of death march through the schedule. Nobody was going to beat me. I had eighteen first-period pins in a row, which set an NCAA record, and finished with twenty-nine pins overall (with twenty-three coming in the first period). I pinned through the Cliff Keen and the Southern Scuffle in-season tournaments and pinned a who's who of all-Americans. I posted a 42–0 overall record, ending with a match in the NCAA finals against Pittsburgh's undefeated Keith Gavin.[30] I beat him 8–2 to win a second national title and took home a second Hodge Trophy, becoming only the second collegiate wrestler to achieve that behind only the great Cael Sanderson.

It was during that final tournament the "Funky" nickname that stayed with me through my MMA career truly came into existence. My buddy Marcus Hoehn had come over sometime early that winter with a T-shirt that he'd made, featuring my face under a pile of hair that made me look like a sponge. Above the image was the word FUNKY straight across the chest. I took

29 We had it working that year. Max was outstanding but had a really bad NCAAs, going 0–2, and Mizzou as a team came in third. Matt Pell came in third in the 165-pound class, winning the Gorrarian Award, which is awarded to the college wrestler with the most pins in the least amount of time in a national tournament.

30 Gavin was an undefeated NCAA champion in 2008 and a Hodge Trophy runner-up.

one look at it and said, "Hey, let's make a whole bunch of those and sell them at the NCAAs." I was cunning, see, because you can't make money as an NCAA athlete...but once it's over, and you win the whole damn thing, you can do whatever you want. He made about five hundred of them. He and about a dozen buddies wore those T-shirts in the stands during the tournament to advertise them, getting shown on the JumboTron and on ESPN. Everybody wanted one. Right after I beat Gavin to win my second title, I was no longer a college athlete. We walked around the parking lot right in Auburn Hills, Michigan, hawking those shirts. It was brilliant.

The shirt was humorous and it made us some cash, but I didn't love the nickname. I tried to ditch it when I started my MMA career a couple of years later, but it followed me like a cult from the mats to the cage. *"Funky"* Ben Askren. Once something like that sticks, you just live with it.[31]

When I look back at my college career at Mizzou, I see it as a night-and-day transformation—the kind of thing I couldn't have achieved with Coach Davis in Wisconsin or anywhere else. I innovated all the way through my college career, and I couldn't have done that without the right coaches and team around me. I had to figure out how to thrive rather than just survive, or—worse yet—fail altogether. Things got dark early on, but when I go back and watch myself as a freshman and compare it to what I'd become by my senior year, it's a world of difference. There are some commonalities interwoven, but it's two different people. I can see the innovations I fished out of myself, and I can remember everything that happened in between as I tried to get better each time out. People ask me sometimes if there was an epiphanic moment when I realized I'd cracked the code, or figured it out.

The answer is no, not really—not the style, anyway. It was a style, but it wasn't the style that got it done. I wasn't out there to prove my style was the best, it was what I had to do

---

31   Now it's even the title of this fucking book.

to be the best, and I clung to what was working. The puzzle for me was figuring out a way to implement the scrambling, and that meant years of trial and error. I just wanted to win, and the numbers live on in the record books in Columbia. I was 153–8 in college wrestling. I went 87–0 through my junior and senior years, winning two titles and two Hodge Trophies. I finished with 91 falls and 771 dual points. Whether Coach Smith called me before that Fargo tournament to come to Missouri or after, it's all history—I'm just glad he called. Mizzou wrestling has been rolling along ever since.

After doing everything in my power to leave a mark on college wrestling, there was only one thing left on my mind: make the 2008 Olympic team. That goal, which had been with me the whole way, was all that mattered.

CHAPTER FOUR:
OLYMPIC DREAMS

"Arriving at one goal is the starting point to another."

–John Dewey

There was a kid I helped out in high school named Richie Dunn. He was younger than me by a few years, and for all intents and purposes, he was a terrible wrestler. He just didn't seem to have it. When I went off to college he continued to work at it as hard as he could and by degrees got better and better over the next couple of years. By the time he was a senior at Arrowhead he was competing for the state title.

I drove back to Wisconsin from Missouri to see him compete, and—against all odds from where he started—he freaking won. Richie Dunn had dedicated himself toward doing something that early on didn't seem in the cards, and he did it. If Dunn wasn't a testament to what commitment, hard work, and self-belief mean for wrestling, I don't know who is. I was very proud of him, and he had every reason to celebrate that feat.

Yet, standing with him afterward, as he was soaking it all in, I asked him, "What's next?" I don't remember his response. I think he sat there kind of blank, as if it hadn't occurred to him that there had to be something next. What I do remember is that kid feeling on top of the world about what he'd just accomplished, something he'd dedicated himself to for countless hours for years, not sure how to respond. He had probably wanted me, a mentor, to recognize just how far he'd come. But there I was asking him, "What's next?"

What a dumb thing to say. Why wasn't I just letting him enjoy his moment? This was a kid who never thought he was going to achieve that, and then there I was asking him what's next, as if winning a state title wasn't good enough, as if there had to be a bigger-picture progression he was working toward, beyond winning a freaking state title. All these years later it hurts me to remember it, as it's something that I mentally replay from time to time.

If anything, I discovered something at that moment about how my mind works. For me, having an Olympic dream meant all the other things—high school, regional tournaments, college, international tournaments—were like hurdles to clear in reaching that goal. Each stop was big, but I was in a constant state of leveling up, achieving one thing, fighting through whatever adversities got in my way, then going for the next. I'd been working for a dozen years, often training two times a day, and all of it was headed to Beijing. In that forward-thinking mindset, winning high school and college titles wasn't my destiny. My destiny was to represent America in wrestling. I was somewhat single-minded in that pursuit, and it was like a decade-long obstacle course to get there. I can distinctly remember being asked in a Q&A with the *Columbia Tribune* toward the end of my time at Mizzou if I was good enough to make the Olympics.[32]

"No," I said, as it is my compulsion to be as honest as possible—a trait that has gotten me into hot water at times. "But I think I will be shortly."

Everything had a next. Everything I had done through college had been building toward the 2008 Summer Olympics, going back to Dallas when I was a kid in awe of those

---

32 Cleverly entitled "the Ben Commandments."

participating in the trials. Everything I did I'd kept in context to that end. In 2005, I had taken fourth at the World Team Trials, and I scored a victory over Andy Hrovat, who, somewhat shockingly, ended up beating Mo Lawal to make the 2008 Olympic team. I knew he was an Olympic-caliber wrestler when I beat him. These things matter when you're climbing closer to something. Such associations have special meaning.

In 2006 I can remember helping Team Wisconsin, which my brother Max was on. For whatever reason, USA Wrestling held a senior level training camp alongside the Junior Nationals, which afforded me a unique opportunity. I was able to wrestle and I beat Joe Williams in a practice match, who was a longtime US representative at 74kg (163 pounds)—a weight I had been contemplating dropping down to. He had taken fourth in the 2004 Olympics in Athens, and that registered with me in huge ways. I was an Olympic aspirant beating an Olympic veteran, which was a big boost for my confidence. After that match with Williams, I made the decision to go down to 74kg. I hadn't weighed 163 pounds since high school. I'd filled in considerably since then, so it wasn't my ideal weight class by any means. But it was a new challenge. Though I don't have an addictive personality, the way I gravitated toward challenges bordered on addiction.

I finished college in March 2007, and I was faced with a decision: Do I keep competing until the Olympic Trials, which were still a year off? Or do I look to capitalize in other ways? If I'm being honest, there was also a wild sense of liberation that spring—this urge to switch gears right then and there. Having accomplished what I did in college, there was a temptation to segue straight into mixed martial arts, where I could arrive with a certain amount of juice as a two-time Hodge winner. There was money in MMA, far bigger money than I could make doing wrestling tournaments. It was booming. People were in my ear. And having a wrestling base in MMA had proven over time to be crucial, with guys like Randy Couture, who'd wrestled at Oklahoma State as a three-time all-American, holding the UFC's heavyweight title. Many MMA champions were wrestlers first. I felt I could be too. I gave it serious consideration, because I wanted to make sure whatever I decided I would dedicate myself to 100 percent.

Of course, some of these thoughts of transitioning to MMA and foregoing the Olympics had to do with the 74kg weight class. To make that weight would require me to whittle down my weight like a yogi, essentially refitting myself into a different frame. I knew it would be hard. Very hard. Yet I did what I knew I would do all along. I started slowly shedding the weight. And, as had been the theme of my competitive life, I was in for some early sorrows.

The first tournament at my new weight class after my college career was the US Open in 2007, where I entered as a seven seed. I would soon find out the tolls my body was taking for cutting all that weight. I won the first two matches, including a match against the two-seed Tyrone Lewis. I felt pretty good until I went up against Joe Heskett, who'd wrestled at Iowa State, in the next round in the semifinals. I won the first period, but this was a best two-out-of-three setup,[33] and in the second period my legs felt like they were in mud, like I was literally pulling them out of suck holes. They weren't obeying my mind's commands at all. In that third match, after the shock of such an immense weight cut, my body quit on me. I had nothing left, and Heskett beat me the next two periods to win.

Inevitably, I lost the last match I competed in to Wisconsin's own Donny Pritzlaff, who was a world bronze medalist in 2006. Pritzlaff was an important rival to me, in part because he was somebody I looked up to at the University of Wisconsin, and in part because he was a good litmus test to see where I was. Not being able to give him my best that day bothered me.

It would be a slow acclimation to get comfortably down to 163 pounds. In the World Trials that same year, I lost to Donny

---

33 Which was an incredibly stupid rule set.

again on the front side in the semis. That was rough in itself, but losing to Ramico Blackmon stung a great deal more.[34] This was a guy I knew I should beat. I ended up taking fifth and sixth place at those two events—the US Open and the Worlds—which was a million miles from where I needed to be. To make the Olympic team, I'd need to be No. 1. The distance between fifth/sixth and first in the trials is the gulf between playing Double-A ball and being in the Major Leagues, and I had only a year to close that gap.

This is where my fascination with sports psychology— especially as I could step outside myself and view my situation from an unemotional place—paid off yet again. Having been through competitive adversity at so many junctures of my career served me well that summer, as I reasoned to myself that I was still getting used to competing at such a smaller weight. I was walking around somewhere between 172–175 pounds, which was as lean as my body could get. The struggles were a symptom of all the change.

I was also adapting my style once again, transitioning from the folkstyle—that I'd essentially workshopped and innovated in order to swing things in my favor in college—to freestyle. The main issue was my baseline defense with my legs. In college I'd been able to use scrambling to find my way out of a lot of trouble situations, but with the scoring dynamics of freestyle it became much harder. I needed to dial things back a bit and crush the basics.

That summer of 2007 there weren't any tournaments to partake in, so I worked on managing my weight and the fundamentals of wrestling. In the fall I wrestled in the Sunkist Kids Open in Phoenix, Arizona.[35] Though I felt a little more comfortable with the weight, it was ultimately another disappointment. I came in fourth place after a fairly strong start. Once again, I found myself fading as the tournament went on. But there was progress, and sometimes that is all you need. It's in these strug-

---

34 Blackmon would go on to have a fairly decent run in MMA.
35 Sunkist was a major sponsor of the US Team.

gles that you live and ultimately thrive as a competitor. You fail, you work harder; you come up short again, you keep going, you succeed. You keep a strict perspective on everything so as to not let yourself off the hook during triumphs, and you resolve to fix things that didn't work during setbacks.

In watching Olympic athletes, I know there have been a million doubts that have tried to derail them, privately and publicly, that can never be fully expressed. What you're seeing with high-level athletes is stubbornness and perseverance at work. They have made an art form of thankless repetition and tedium.

Stamina, which had been my most ruthless and reliable strong suit in college, was still an issue. My mind had plans that my body wasn't able to accommodate, and this was the little private war that took place until late that year at the New York Athletic Club Open.

That's when things started falling into place.

I broke through and won the NYAC, which was a big one, and, perhaps more significantly, I was able to overcome Donny Pritzlaff. He had been my nemesis over the last year, the hurdle I couldn't seem to clear, so beating somebody that good was another marker of my progress. Then, a couple of weeks later, I won the Hargobind in Vancouver. I finished up that one by beating none other than Ramico Blackmon, the guy I'd lost to at the US Open. I wasn't fading down the stretch anymore. I had begun to inhabit my new weight comfortably. The technical adjustments and tweaks I'd made were working, too. I was getting back a couple of those losses, and I was locking in at the right time. As I'd done my junior and senior years of college, I started winning.

And I didn't stop.

I went overseas to get some international experience, a kind of final tune-up for the stretch run toward the Open and trials. The first bit of business came in February at the World Cup in a place called Vladikavkaz, Russia, which is at the seat of the Caucasus Mountains. It was a crazy first experience on the international scene. This place was about as Russian as Russia gets. Cold, jagged, stern-feeling, steely, it had all the humor and warmth of beet borscht.

Years later, I did a little promo video in the lead-up to a pay-per-view boxing exhibition with Jake Paul in which I reenacted the *Rocky IV* training montage—chopping wood, pulling my kids on a sled, running through snow up a hillside—as Rocky trained in Russia for Drago. While doing that, I kept thinking back to Vladikavkaz, right there on the Terek River in the heart of our Cold War counterpart.

It was my first real taste of international competition, and I went 3–1 in the tournament. I lost to a Russian wrestler named Denís Tsargúsh, who went on to be a three-time world champion and took home bronze in the 2012 Olympics in London. Tsargúsh was a good wrestler, but he was a filthy bastard, and everyone knew he was a notorious cheater. He ripped chunks of my hair out during that match in Russia. He grabbed a clump of hair and then single-legged the other side, a little pull-and-go maneuver. There was a nest of my hair lying on the mat that he had yanked straight off my scalp. I didn't speak Russian, but I pointed to that incriminating hank of hair to the referee, a gesture that needed no interpreter, but he just shrugged his shoulders and insinuated to keep wrestling. I was like, guess that's not against the rules.

That was my introduction to international wrestling.

But I scored some good victories in Russia, too. I beat a guy from the Ukraine, who was really good, and another solid wrestler from Turkey. I was as loose as ever, same unorthodox, carefree "Funky" Askren that Eastern Europeans might find grating. My easy vibe was at odds with the terrain. Even there in Russia—or especially in Russia—my free-spiritedness was considered both cocky and disarming, which annoyed the hell out of people.

A week later on that same trip I went to Kiev for another tournament, this time taking third in what turned into one of those infamous international experiences that I'd heard about from other wrestlers. I did fine, all told, but the one match I lost was a robbery. Competitively speaking, I was literally robbed. I was winning the match against a Ukrainian wrestler with six seconds left in the match. I'm thinking, *Okay, six seconds, I'll just move around a bit, whatever, burn those last ticks off the clock.* We started wrestling, and time goes by. And it keeps going, though the clock remained still, to the point that I'm thinking, *How fucking long does six seconds take*? Just having a thought like that cross your mind takes six seconds, yet the clock wasn't going.

I yell to my coach, "Hey, they didn't start the clock," and he yells over to the officials. Now, I'm distracted, and, at that precise moment, during this absurd sequence, with my focus pulled two ways, I ended up getting taken down to lose the match. Mysteriously, just as my body hit the mat, the clock began running again as if time itself had been patiently waiting for the momentum to change.

Naturally, I protested, pointing out, ever so politely, that what just happened was fucking bullshit![36] So the officials there rewound the tape to where the clock actually started—not to when we actually began wrestling—and then counted...one... two...three...four...five...six. They came back with, "Yeah, the match is over—that was six seconds." There was some serious home cooking going on in Kiev.

But I couldn't complain overall. I went a combined 8–2 in my first international tournaments, even with being cheated. I felt pretty good about how I sized up with the international competition, and I made a vow right then to braid my hair next time through.

I carried that momentum to the 2008 US Open in April— just a couple of months before the Olympic Trials—which I entered as the third seed. I thought I should be higher since I'd won the NYAC Open and the Hargobind, but I didn't dwell on it. Instead, I funneled everything through the mats. I killed

---

36   There's a reason I am using this kind of language here, and that's because it was fucking bullshit.

Ramico Blackmon to kick things off and was supposed to face Donny Pritzlaff in the next round, but he ended up losing. I drew Ryan Churella instead, a guy who'd lost dramatically in the final seconds to Johny Hendricks in the 2006 NCAA finals while wrestling with Michigan. I was able to get through Churella pretty easily, setting myself up for a match in the finals against Tyrone Lewis.

Lewis had been a beast at Oklahoma State, he was super tough, but I beat him in two periods to win the Open and qualify for the Olympic Trials. That was a much better result than the previous year; I felt like I was hitting my stride. I'd had to get used to the period system that was used in these tournaments, but once I started rounding that corner I was dominant, right where I knew I had to be. Out of a total thirty-three periods during that stretch, I lost just one. This was the turning point for me because I'd never really been a sprinter throughout my career. I'd been a slow starter. It had always taken me some time to get into the match. So, for me, especially that first year, to win the first two-minute period in a match was the challenge, and I'd been able to do that at the Open.

Now it was time for the Olympic Trials, which were held in Las Vegas at the Thomas & Mack Center. I was so locked in that I didn't consider anything other than winning. Yet, after making a small fortune selling the FUNKY T-shirts at the NCAAs, I wasn't about to let a big event like the trials go by without capitalizing with a little self-promotion.

I went back to my same buddy who'd made those shirts and had him print up a new one that said, "Putting the Chin in China," which featured my mashed face in profile with a big chin silhouetted against the Chinese flag. As far as self-promotion at that time in my life, that was a big venture. Again, I was doing things my way, which were a little different than the wrestling community was used to. Selling promo T-shirts presumed—somewhat cockily, I admit—I'd be headed to China. Nobody had done that kind of thing before. I had a section of fans wearing these, and it pissed off some of the competitors at the Thomas & Mack.

I relished it. I was having fun with things, but I was seriously locked in.

As a kid, I had magnified the "big" moments to the point that it affected my performance. Heading into the trials, I was respectful of the field but not in awe. As far as I was concerned, everything went through me. I saw a familiar cast of characters, too, from the nuisances to the rivals. I got through Blackmon again and this time got to face off with Pritzlaff in the next tier. It was a memorable encounter.

One of the reasons that I came up short early on in freestyle was because of the rules themselves. They sucked. I wasn't a fan of them. If you went through two minutes and it was 0-0, you went to something called the "ball grab." They would place a red ball and a blue ball in a bag and draw to determine who would get a starting position from the bottom and who would get the other's leg. If you drew the ball that gave you the leg, you were in a really advantageous position. The ratio of people winning from that position was like 90 percent. It wasn't 60/40, it was literally 90/10—very stacked in that lucky, completely arbitrary ball-winner's favor.

So one of the things I'd practiced over and over was being in that specific position, because I knew that—once people realized I was better than them—they could always hope to stall out for two minutes and force that situation. You weren't penalized for stalling in freestyle, which left things open for competitive gaming; they'd stall, get to the ball grab and, if fortune shined on them, get my leg, thus swinging the odds their favor.

For some wrestlers I knew this was the best strategy to beat me. Understanding that, I practiced every single day having someone start with my leg. The idea was to thwart, to prevent them from pushing you with your leg in the air. I would take the lesser position, time and again, repeat, repeat, repeat, trying to balance and not get taken down. It paid off.

Pritzlaff got my leg in the first ten seconds of the match, and he spent a full minute trying to do something with it, yet he couldn't take me down and he couldn't push me out. I knew. I could feel it. He literally gave up after that. There's a term we use in wrestling: "breaking." I felt Donny break the moment I got my foot back on the mat. I scored immediately and it was all downhill from there, and I won the first period 3–0. I had felt this many times in high school when opponents were overmatched, many times in college; in a dictation of wills, which is what wrestling is at its core, it's the ultimate satisfaction to break a competitor. I don't know if it was that he realized there wasn't any hope or if he just got frustrated, but he broke in that semifinals match. There would be no ball grab.

Just like at the US Open, I drew Tyrone Lewis in the finals in what was a best two-out-of-three series. I had done a very amateurish braid job in haste at the hotel, specifically because I knew from experience that Lewis (not unlike Tsargúsh) liked to pull hair. With my trademark locks, the hair was just too tempting. He'd seize it by the fistful if I didn't take the option away.

I beat Lewis two periods to zero in the first match, and it wasn't all that competitive. Then in the second one he actually threw me onto my back in the first period, which was a jolt. In the heat of competition, control and chaos can become interchangeable. But that was not how I envisioned things happening. I had to compete off my back and fight my ass off to get back up, which I ultimately did, but I was down one period to nothing.

It was the only period I lost to an American since the Sunkist tournament. I came back and beat him relatively soundly in periods two and three to clinch. In the narrow focus of the trials, in the monotonous way I was countering every offensive and preempting every stall, I kept the carrot in my peripheral vision. In my singular, granular focus to outlast the other, to score, to dominate, to not survive but thrive, I didn't dare look at it directly.

Now I could look at it directly. After a decade of work, of weight cutting and perseverance, of overruling my every doubt and adapting at every level, I had done it. After dreaming of this moment for so long, and working toward it relentlessly, obsessively, and religiously, I had achieved the ultimate "next."

I made the Olympic team.

I had made it.

People who knew just how hard I'd worked over the years would ask me what it felt like. Elation? Euphoria? Cloud nine? It's difficult to describe, because so much of the journey was inward and personal, and the emotions tied to something like that are stronger than basic language can convey. It's a feeling you don't get much in life. Even in fighting years later, nothing I ever did matched those feelings. After working toward a goal for so long, you get this overwhelming feeling of relief that you've somehow realized it. After betting on yourself for so long, it's a confirmation of belief. All at once you can do away with opinions on the subject of whether or not you're good enough.

At that point, you are.

I would say there are three or four times in my life I've felt something like that so wholly. Winning the state title in high school was one. The match I won to get my college scholarship. The first national title at Mizzou. Each of those was huge and carried something of an absolute in terms of satisfaction. But making the Olympic team was where I'd always hoped—where I'd always believed—it was all headed. The first Mizzou Tiger wrestler to make it. The punk kid from Hartland. The object of all that message-board hate.

I am not a crier, but I remember telling a reporter from ESPN that it didn't hit me until I talked to a group of six hundred kids at a team camp back at Mizzou and explained how I'd got there, how after reflecting on all the years of toil I went to my car and broke down. I cried.

But I am a pragmatist at heart, and I didn't have much time to revel in it. That was June 18, and the opening ceremonies for the Olympics in Beijing were scheduled for August 8, with a departure date to Beijing almost a week before that. Those six weeks passed by at warp speed, and during that super-condensed window I had to switch gears from thinking about zeroing in on beating out my American counterparts to figuring out how to beat the world's best wrestlers that awaited.

These days it's a lot different, with so much more coverage and so much more time between the trials and the Games and so many more ways to scout competition. I wasn't afforded that luxury then. I had a matter of weeks. I couldn't put a high amount of focus on the international playing field—on how to beat this guy or that guy—like I had with my domestic competition. I just had to make sure I was showing up as the best version of myself, ready to deal with any-and-everything that I might encounter.

To prepare, I trained with Max and the Sunkist Kids—myself, Henry Cejudo, Daniel Cormier, Andy Hrovat, and Steve Mocco—down in Phoenix, in the Arizona State wrestling room. Doug Schwab and Mike Zadick, who rounded out the US Team out of the University of Iowa, had opted to hang back in Iowa City.

The team got along very well together, for the most part. Personally, I hit it off with Daniel the best. He had a way of bullying the other guys in nonthreatening, non-mean-spirited ways, and he liked nothing more than to push people's buttons.[37] I think he liked me because I gave it right back to him. Some of the other guys were a little more reserved and timid, not knowing how to take his constant ribbing, but he couldn't get to me. I didn't give a damn and—as a natural antagonist myself—had thick, impenetrable skin. I was always willing to fire right back at him, and we formed a great rapport that remains intact to this day.

---

37 Anybody who has followed his storied MMA career knows exactly what I'm talking about.

Phoenix was the first of two mini-ten-day training camps, with the second being held a few days later down at altitude at the Olympic Training Center in Colorado Springs, this time with the whole US Team in attendance. It didn't feel like cramming for worldly competition, but the summer had turned into a kind of mad, hyper-focused dash toward this grand pageant in some abstract, far-off land. All those years dreaming about the Olympics, and now here I was, rolling with Max—just like we did back in Wisconsin as kids in the family basement—in preparation for Beijing on a rapidly moving conveyor belt toward the biggest moment of my life.

We did our staging near San Jose, California, getting sized for our clothes and taking care of all the formalities. They give you a shopping cart, and you try on a bunch of shit—Nike and Ralph Lauren were the two big sponsors, as I recall—and they filled up your cart. I am not a big fan of clothes in general, nor of name brands. Shorts, sandals, and a T-shirt are all I need to feel dressed; the less I have to wear, the better. Everybody knows what my bare feet look like. So I ended up giving about 85 percent of the gear they gave me to friends and family. They bused us all to San Francisco, and as a squad we had a flight chartered to Beijing.

From there it was all kind of a blur but also—being an impatient person—almost like a purgatorial sentence I had to endure before competition. Time moved slowly when I became aware of it. I'd never been to China before, so the whole experience was new to me. I remember getting to the Olympic village, the whole pomp and circumstance surrounding that, and checking out the athletic dining halls. Everything for the athletes was in one place, which made it feel familiar pretty quickly. At Beijing University they'd staged all our training partners and coaches, like an American training post with all the mats and weights. It was a nice setup. I did some tourist things to pass the time. I shopped around. I made it out to the Great Wall of China. I watched my fellow Olympians compete and win gold medals, making the most of their moments. Michael Phelps was collecting gold like an early prospector. I'd put on movies, including the quintessential wrestling movie, *Vision Quest*, which everybody assumes wrestlers love. Bullshit. I'd never realized just how terrible it was until watching it in China. Total 1980s sentimental crap.

Maybe the highlight of the experience was the opening ceremonies. It was a dream come true. That's when it hit me in full, when I could sit back and look at the size of it, this celebrated microcosmos. I felt great, my weight was on point, my mindset was right—I felt 100 percent sure I would bring home gold. The media was eating it up, because I was very laid back. I think a lot of people saw me as this carefree Midwestern guy who was always smiling like I was in on a joke, irreverent, and completely unaffected by the magnitude of the event.

To be honest, they weren't far off. I was loose. I was ready.

A couple of days before I was to wrestle, I did what all my fans from college might've considered a form of blasphemy: I went and got my hair cut. I had several inches cut off to thwart hair-pullers like Tsargúsh from any sordid temptation. Since this was the culmination of all I had worked for, I sacrificed my hair as one might a lamb in some darker ritual. My trademark, my identity, the Funky 'Fro that ESPN had mythologized during the NCAAs...gone. I had cut it down to cafeteria-lady length.

Not that many people thought I'd win, anyway.

I had a rabid fanbase, but the odds were stacked against me. They had me installed at twenty-to-one to bring home gold heading in at my weight class. A long shot. The favorite, the two-time-winning gold medalist Buvaisar Saitiev from Russia, loomed over everyone. His name was mentioned at each gathering, whispered all over the mats, and he was on the cusp of becoming the best of all time. Then there was Iván Fundora from Cuba, a thirty-two-year-old wrestling icon who'd picked up a bronze medal in Athens four years earlier and who, by comparison, had a lifetime of international experience.

I had two international tournaments to my name. The wrestling program that was distributed to provide spectators background on our collective achievements didn't even bother mentioning me among the notables. In fact, they reserved only a single line for me: "Ben Askren is an outspoken young wrestler with limited international experience."

That's it. Eleven words.

Naturally, I ate it up. I was twenty-four years old and had realized a dream, which was to get the opportunity to represent my country. I knew who I was and what I could do. As the underdog, there was a Cinderella feeling to my placement, too. My light vibe was one of possibility. There was an air of a live dog, a wild card to the whole thing that wasn't intimidated by the Saitievs or the Soslan Tigievs.

The next ceremony I attended wasn't nearly as fun, nor as surreal. It was the blind draw to determine our place in the brackets.

They don't go in for seeding in the Olympics, which means it's luck of the draw.[38] I thought the worst matchup for me heading in was the Cuban Fundora, because he was so good defensively. Fundamentally, I could see how he might nullify some of my offensive output and that he'd be a handful. I drew No. 14, meaning I was out of the running for a bye and would have to face Fundora in the second round if I beat my first opponent, István Veréb of Hungary. Equally harrowing, I'd have to face Saitiev in the following round, making my road to gold about as difficult as they come.

So be it, I thought. *You deal with what you're dealt.*

The China Agricultural University Gymnasium was alive with everything I'd imagined as a kid. There were world-class wrestlers and coaches around me. The media. My brother Max was there; so was my soon-to-be wife, who'd just flown in. My coaches, Shawn Charles and John Mesenbrink, who'd been with me the whole way in preparation for the Olympics, were

---

38 Or at least they didn't, the great wisdom of the IOC finally added seeding in 2021.

there too as we made our way in. I had a little Askren booster club of about twenty-five to thirty people, most wearing Afro wigs and waving the American flag. Throughout all the buildup, I'd been the picture of calm, which I'd heard time and again was refreshing. So many athletes were like tension rods in Beijing, in stark contrast to my loose demeanor. But why not? The size of the moment was just an abstraction now. I wasn't actively minimizing pressure. I was doing what I had learned all those years ago in Fargo.

I was treating the Olympics like any other event.

Veréb held the distinction of being the only other wrestler younger than me in my weight class, and I thought it would be beneficial to get a warm-up match in before facing Fundora and Saitiev. As usual, I got off to a slow start. Veréb struck me with two quick takedowns, and right away I was down 2–0. The thought flashed through my mind: Am I in over my head?

But by the end of the first two-minute period, I could already feel him wilting. In the second period I scored right away, and I could feel him break. I scored an easy takedown and sensed the fight was going out of him, then locked up one of my patented cradles off a scramble and decked him.

It was a solid start. It felt great to get the day rolling in the right direction, but now I'd have to face Fundora less than half an hour later. I predicted he was the worst possible matchup for me, and he was, and he showed that in the first period. He got my legs and was able to power through, winning it 3–1. I can remember the rooting section coming to life. They'd seen me come back before. They knew I was in it. Those closest to me, who'd made the trip overseas thousands of miles to see me compete, believed in me.

In the second period, I upped the urgency. I shouldn't have started forcing stuff, but I did. I forced stuff that really wasn't there. I got frustrated because I just couldn't open him up, and it backfired on me. It was one of my worst performances ever, because I was wrestling uncharacteristically. He got up 2–0 in the second period, then 4–0.

It was over.

As it sank in, all I could do was stand there and exhale. So that was how it would end. I wasn't out of the medal running, but I might as well have been. The way it works in the Olympics is you only get a chance to take third if the guy you lose to goes on to the finals. It's a format called "follow the leader," and it's really stupid in my opinion.

Fundora was going up against the two-time Olympic gold winner Saitiev.[39] That meant my fate—and my chance at a bronze—was now hitched to Fundora pulling off an upset. Given that, I knew I was out. A bystander about to watch all those years add up to heartbreak. There's only one thing worse than not being in control of your own fate: giving it away to begin with. I was powerless to do anything. My medal was tied to something no longer in my control, which for me was Fundora.[40] It was hell.

He lost. I was out of the tournament. My Olympics were over. There was a deeply hollow feeling that I felt walking off the mats. I had been obsessing for a decade on going to the Olympics, which only comes around every four years, but I hadn't given much thought to walking away empty-handed. Such is the strength of belief. Now that I had, I was somewhat rudderless in China, devoid of feeling but also not ready to make excuses. That's the one thing I didn't want to do.

"I don't know what you want to hear from me," I said when asked what was next afterwards by the media. "My dreams are crushed. I just wasn't good enough. I sucked."

I was twenty-four years old. What was next?

The year 2012 was a lifetime away. Redemption in the Olympics was such a remote possibility in those deflating moments. After giving it your all and winning or giving it your everything and

---

39   Soon to be three-time Olympic gold winner.
40   I wrestled him two years later in a tournament in Havana and stuck to the game plan I should have stuck to in Beijing, which was to be more patient and force him into mistakes. I beat him.

coming up short, either way those two words have no meaning.

What's next.

Nobody wants to hear that when the only future you've ever known suddenly becomes the past.

CHAPTER FIVE:
SEGUE INTO MMA

"Your daddy fights tigers."

—My wife, Amy, to our daughter Alex, who was curious as to what her dad did for a living

There are a million stories about how people got into cagefighting, which became a thing in 1993 when the UFC put on an eight-man "no holds barred" tournament in Denver. Mostly they saw VHS tapes long after the fact and were drawn to the raw, bootleg nature of such an extreme spectacle. The idea of dropping a bunch of guys from different martial arts backgrounds—boxing, wrestling, jiu-jitsu, savate, sumo—into the same tournament was like a real-life version of *Bloodsport*, and it spoke directly to anyone who engaged in combat sports.

Fifteen years later, in 2008, when MMA was well aboveground and booming, the early players were cult figures. Royce Gracie was a legend by then. So were guys like Don Frye and Dan Severn, former collegiate wrestlers who found a natural segue in cagefighting. I remember my dad bringing home one of the early UFCs from 1993 or 1994—back when they were marketing the ridiculous "two men enter, one man leaves" angle—and thinking it was all pretty crazy.

I have this memory of a guy punching a piece of cement in a promo clip they ran from one of the originals UFCs. His hands were duct-taped, and he was pounding away at this cement as if to demonstrate what a lunatic he was. It was the fringes-of-society vibe the early UFC was selling, but all I remember thinking was, *Why is this idiot hitting cement? Nobody has to do that. How completely moronic.* But those types of roadhouse personalities seemed to find their way to cagefighting.

Some of the early bouts grabbed my attention, and I developed loose rooting interests. I didn't really like guys like Ken Shamrock, who was strutting around back then, but I remember watching Kevin Randleman and Bas Rutten go at it in UFC 20. That fight really stood out to me, but I was never too obsessed with it. I just thought it was something taboo to rent.

It wasn't until 2005, when *The Ultimate Fighter* came out, that I got reeled in in a bigger way. That was the UFC's reality television vehicle that stuck a bunch of fighters in a house with fully stocked liquor cabinets, the hook being a tournament to win a "six-figure contract" with the UFC.[41] The Forrest Griffin–Stephan Bonnar finale was, at the time, a thunderbolt for MMA. A lot of people were paying attention to the fight as it aired live on Spike TV, and the fight, which featured no defense whatsoever and very little in the way of anything resembling self-preservation,[42] delivered in a big way. I think Dana White has called it the "Trojan Horse" that busted the UFC into American living rooms and, at least, dropped it off on the outskirts of mainstream sports.

I'd been contemplating a career in MMA, but it was always more of a horizon thought—something to give serious consideration to *after* the Olympics. I felt it would be a natural transition for me, and I knew I could continue competing as an athlete at a high level while making money. As much as I wanted it to be otherwise, there wasn't any money in wrestling.

---

41 Of course they didn't mention that the six figures would be spread over multiple fights, thus tying a fighter to the semi-long term on the cheap.

42 In other words, the perfect UFC fight to create a major buzz.

In December 2006, during my final season at Mizzou, I'd made a visit to Las Vegas and asked the assistant coach, Bart Horton, if we could take the van down to talk with Randy Couture.[43] Randy was a champion in MMA, one of the biggest names at the time in the UFC and a former wrestler himself. Asking Coach Horton was strategic. If I'd asked Coach Smith to take me to meet Randy to discuss MMA, I knew he would just say, "Yeah right." But Horton was my guy, a coach who eased the tension in competition and ended up becoming a really close friend and confidant. I knew he'd go along with it.

Randy ran through the pros and cons of going into MMA, which is when the seeds were starting to get planted. I was getting more and more into MMA as time went on. During my time at Mizzou, my college buddies and I would rent old PRIDE FC and UFC DVDs, and I really enjoyed watching them, so much so that I attended a couple of events and meetings in person.

In October 2006, I flew down to Hollywood, Florida, to see the trilogy fight between Tito Ortiz and Ken Shamrock, which was held on a rare Tuesday night. I really got into the bad blood between those guys, and it was fun to watch Tito smash Shamrock in the first round. In March 2008, I attended UFC 82 in Columbus, Ohio, when Dan Henderson, a tough Greco-Roman fighter who was a two-division champion in PRIDE, took on Anderson Silva for the middleweight belt. Henderson came out to Red Rider's "Lunatic Fringe," a song from that shitty wrestling movie, *Vision Quest*, and it brought the crowd in Columbus to its feet. I had attended that fight with a guy I thought might be a potential manager for me in MMA, so the thoughts about MMA were taking shape in (still somewhat hypothetical) stages.

In fact, in between these events, during the weekend of the US Open in 2007, I met up with the guys at Team Take-

43 Thinking about it, this might've been an NCAA violation. But screw it. Nothing can be done about that now.

down to discuss the possibility of joining up. Team Take-down, which eventually became the hub team of wrestlers like Johny Hendricks, Shane Roller, and Jake Rosholt, had a unique setup that offered fighters a salary of somewhere between $60,000 and $100,000, along with health insurance, housing, and a car, with the catch being that the fighter would then split his fight purses with management 50/50. In the back of my head, I was pondering all this.

After coming up short in the Olympics, I needed to let things fall off my shoulders. For so long I'd been in pursuit of a singular goal; it was liberating to have a future unfolding in front of me with no definitive destination.

When I returned home to Wisconsin, I took a little time off. I embarked on a road trip to Austin, Texas, with my friend James Hefner to play as much disc golf as we could while visiting the headquarters of FloWrestling,[44] a brand-new startup site that my pal Martin Floreani had launched. With the relative lack of in-depth amateur wrestling coverage, I was very much into this enterprise—especially with my buddies Mark Bader and Joe Williamson working there as well. As someone who was committed to being an ambassador for wrestling for the rest of my life, I found what FloWrestling was doing vital for the growth of the sport.

Then I took a vacation with my girlfriend—and eventual wife—Amy on a tour of the American Southeast, visiting national parks throughout Kentucky, Tennessee, South Carolina, North Carolina, Virginia, and West Virginia. I saw a lot of old friends on that trip. It was like catching up with everything I hadn't been able to before. The idea was to enjoy myself, reflect, and move forward. Because if I understood anything, it's that defeat would not define me.

If anything, my resiliency would.

It sounds like a stupid cliché, but to be anything in this life means to overcome adversity, time and again. It's not that

---

44 I actually got pretty damn good at disc golf. I took ninth place in the Amateur
    Worlds in both 2009 and 2011, and second in the Amateur Nationals in 2011.

you'll fail, because failure is inevitable; it's how you deal with failure. It's what you do with it. The truth is those who don't (or can't) deal with it well aren't talked about. You'll never hear the stories of those who don't bounce back. The ones you hear about are the resilient people who didn't accept defeat. Elon Musk made it big with PayPal, invested all his money in other things, almost went bankrupt like seventeen times, then made it big again. Much bigger. Each stage was a chapter to his full story. It didn't end at the first failure.

To use the world of wrestling, I knew that just about every well-known wrestler in America had dealt with tremendous adversity. David Taylor? Kyle Dake? J'den Cox? Jordan Burroughs? I can cite exactly where they had their adversity and the exact moment they were forced to fight through. As a competitor, it's something you've got to do. If you don't, you disappear from the great log of human beings that went on to achieve amazing things.

It might be that I'm somewhat on the spectrum—in fact, I've self-diagnosed myself with Asperger's, because I check a lot of the boxes[45]—but I've always been very pragmatic. I overrule unnecessary expenditures of emotion all the time, and you'd never know I was dwelling on any hardship by outward appearances. It's not in my personality type to dwell on the past, in particular, which is something I learned about myself through years of competition. This was in evidence more publicly a decade later in my fight with Jorge Masvidal, which became a meme for millions to try to use against me.

How do you deal with getting knocked out in five seconds, and—in the age of social media—being forced to see the replay a billion times? By remembering the simple fact that life moves in but one direction: forward. It's a waste of time to focus on the past, because you can't change it. My mindset has always been more along the lines of, okay,

---

45 I mean a lot of boxes. Difficulty with nonverbal behavior, like hand gestures and eye contact? Check. Impatience with small talk on trivial matters? Check. Obsession with specific interests? Check. Check. Check.

that happened, that sucked, I didn't like that, but now what? The "now what" is where my focus tends. Overall, I'm more practical than I am emotional.

It was no different as I reflected on my run to the Olympics.

It's a depressing thing because of the cold reality. In fighting, if you work your way to a title and fuck up your chance, you can get another shot in the next couple of months or on the next card—you can remedy the loss quickly. With the Olympics, it's four years, an entire presidential term. I knew there probably wouldn't be another shot, and I knew that in the somewhat nascent world of MMA, which hears a buzzword like "Olympian" and runs with it, that "Olympic wrestler Ben Askren" would carry tremendous weight. MMA was definitely the route.

To be honest, I'd already made up my mind. I remember going to a shitty diner with Amy right after the Olympics and saying, "You know, if I'm going to do MMA it's got to be now. I've been thinking about it for a while, and I might as well try it out. If I find that I'm not good at it, or if for some reason I just don't like it, I can just cross it off the list, knowing it's not for me. In that case, I can go back to wrestling and still have three years until the next Olympics in 2012." There was a fallback in place if I needed it, though I knew once I went into MMA I'd go full force. There was a future there. It had plenty of entrepreneurial benefits. And besides, I knew I could promote myself just as I'd done to a much lesser degree in wrestling, and promotion in MMA is everything.

Once I got home I started preparing to fight, while doing some coaching at Mizzou on the side. I trained daily at the local American Top Team affiliate in Missouri with Kiko France and Dustin Denes, both of whom were Brazilian jiu-jitsu black belts. I spent that fall rolling around on the mats and absorbing as much of the submission grappling game as I could, discovering that I really loved it.[46] I was

---

46   Another aspect of Asperger's is to have extraordinary cognitive or creative abili-
     ty, and to grasp difficult concepts quickly. I was fascinated by jiu-jitsu right away
     and consumed by it.

catching on at a good pace, and with my wrestling ability, I felt pretty sure I could control an opponent and therefore dictate the action in an actual fight.

I was impatient, though, and I wanted to start booking myself into fights right away so that I could start building a professional record. I learned pretty quickly, though, that booking a fight was far easier said than done. Nobody wanted to take on an Olympic wrestler unless they got a decent chunk of change. Everyone we approached kept saying, "Nah, I want $5,000 to fight a wrestler," looking to get compensated for what would, in all likelihood, be a miserable night of work. Five grand doesn't sound like a lot, but it is when starting out. The truth was, nobody wanted to fight me. Wrestlers generally don't have a ton of appeal for fighters on the come up, anyway, because most realize their offense will be completely nullified if they're fighting off their backs. The upside of taking on a two-time Hodge winner was next to nil.

I was nothing but downside.

Because of that my ATT gym mate Jake Hecht and Wade Rome, who owned ATT, hatched the idea to promote our own fight card, on which I could make my professional debut. With MMA freshly legal in the state of Missouri, we held it in my college town of Columbia, where I was very much a campus legend. We called it: Headhunter Productions. Back then, every card had an operating title, and we dubbed the first event "Patriot Act."

Thinking back on it, it was a pretty stacked card, though very difficult to book, given our modest budget. My Mizzou teammate Tyron Woodley, who would go on to become a UFC champion, made his professional debut that night, and Neil Magny, another eventual UFC staple, competed as an amateur. The main event featured UFC veteran Din Thomas, who'd had a couple of memorable victories over Clay Guida and Jeremy Stephens.

I don't remember how we found him, but I faced this guy named Josh Flowers, who was fighting out of Kansas City and had a handful of professional bouts. I knew I was far better than him, because I was pretty good already. I'd been training with accomplished welterweights in the UFC and found that I more than held my own. The preceding months had been nomadic ones. I traveled around to get a feel for different gyms and different looks from the fighters.

I went from American Top Team in Florida to the American Kickboxing Academy in San Jose and had great success against veterans in those places. It was during this time I first rolled with Jorge Masvidal in Coconut Creek, which I talked about in the lead-up to our fight in the UFC years later.[47] When I went to AKA, I rolled with the UFC's No. 2 welterweight at the time, Jon Fitch, and thought, *If I can hang with Jon Fitch, I can hang with anyone.* I was having really good success against guys who were relatively high-level fighters, which, as a test market gauge, was a confidence booster.[48] So, realistically, Josh Flowers wasn't all that intimidating.

Being preoccupied with promoting the show was helpful, too, because I could distract myself from overthinking my first fight. If I'm not multitasking, I feel a little lost. It was a decent debut. I pounded Flowers out in a little over a minute, and just like that I was an undefeated fighter with a pro record.

A little over two months later, in April, we rolled things back—this time with the imaginative title of "Patriot Act II"—and same thing, very difficult to find an opponent who didn't want a fortune on such a rinky-dink show out in Missouri to take an *L* against a decorated wrestler. We unearthed a guy named Mitchell Harris, who had a handful of pro fights,

---

47 I made it public that I had my way with him because I knew he'd get pissed about it. It was so easy to put a thumb in his eye, and I wasn't lying. I did whatever I wanted with Jorge. I didn't even have an MMA fight yet, and I fully dominated him.

48 Another time a year later, Jake Shields invited me to come up and train with him prior to his title fight with Georges St-Pierre. I wouldn't say I got the best of Shields, but we had good rolls—very good gos. He was No. 2 in the world at that time.

and he came bearing red flags. He didn't show up to the weigh-ins the day before. I had a feeling of dread remembering the horror stories of guys like Caín Velasquez who had something like ten fights booked and only two opponents showed up. It's a problem getting guys on the regional scene to keep their appointments.

Fortunately, about twenty minutes after the weigh-ins Harris strolled in, tardy and overweight by five pounds, but I didn't care in the slightest—I needed the fight to get rolling, and I didn't want all that training I was doing to go to waste. I knew I could beat him even if he came in at 185 pounds, or 190 pounds. It wouldn't have mattered either way. I choked him out early in the fight and ran my record to 2–0.

As a co-promoter I was gaining valuable insight into the business of MMA—and MMA promotion, for that matter—at warp speed. Both of those shows lost money. I got a lesson right away in just how hard it is to run a show. It's fucking hard. I remember having a discussion with Hecht and Rome where we came to a unanimous agreement to stop promoting our own shows. Headhunter Promotions came to a quick and unceremonious end.

For my third fight, I put a line out to a couple of promoters I knew, advertising that I'd fight for cheap if anyone could just find me an opponent. That opponent ended up being a guy named Matt Delanoit, a vastly more experienced fighter who, with a 14–6 record, had exactly ten times the amount of fights that I did. The fight was in Des Moines, Iowa, for a promotion called Max Fights, which was associated with FloSports, and with my objective being to pile up some experiences and wins, I took it for the whopping sum of $400. Didn't matter to me. I knew I was better than any regional fighter already and that I was a win or two away from getting into a bigger promotion.

I submitted Delanoit in seventy-five seconds. I threw a single punch, did a high-crotch, choked him out, and then dusted my hands off.

About a month later, in late September 2009, just seven months into my pro MMA career, a representative of Bellator—a relatively new promotion that used a tournament structure that I liked and had decent visibility through their TV deal with Fox Sports—got in touch and asked me if I was interested in making $100,000 for three fights, to include a small signing bonus. I distinctly remember saying, "Well, I just made $400 for my last fight, so $100,000 sounds pretty damn good—let's do it!"

It was exactly the kind of deal I was hoping for.

After acting as my own manager for the first couple of fights, I signed on to be represented by Zinkin Entertainment, and the negotiations with Bellator went super quick. By October, I'd signed on, and I was to make my debut the following April in Bellator's Season Two welterweight tournament.

With my MMA career now rolling in the right direction, I made the (in retrospect very poor) decision to wrestle again in 2009–2010 and to compete in some grappling tournaments. That summer I'd taken a post as an assistant coach at Arizona State in Tempe, Arizona, so I started with the Sunkist International Open in Phoenix, right in my own backyard. I did fairly well there in my first wrestling action since the Olympics fourteen months earlier, before running into my old college rival Chris Pendleton again. I won the Grappling Nationals, which were hosted as part of the same tournament,[49] and followed that up by winning the Grappling Worlds (which I don't really count, since nobody was any good there, though I did beat the eccentric UFC fighter Jacob Volkmann).

As somebody who can't sit still, I thought I could wrestle and do MMA at the same time, but I was being naive. You can't half-ass it with wrestling. I wasn't fully invested, so—though maybe I could rationalize I was sharpening my skill set before the Bellator tournament—I was mostly spinning my wheels. And I was burning it at both ends, to tell the truth, crashing through different cities and ports. I hit the

---

49   I even submitted Shannon Ritch, the old jobber who'd fought like a million MMA bouts in a remarkably unremarkable career, LOL.

mats again at the Hargobind in British Columbia and then won the Dave Schultz Memorial out in Colorado in February. Then I went down to Cuba and did the Cerro Pelado—where I exacted a little revenge on Iván Fundora, the Cuban who derailed me in Beijing—before heading over to Belarus to do the Medved, named after the great Aleksandr Medved of Bulgaria in early March 2010.

It was in Belarus, as part of Team USA—just four weeks before my first bout in Bellator—that I broke my finger off. Or, I should say, I somewhat grotesquely mangled my right ring finger in a practice session, which left anybody who saw it in mute horror. The finger came out of the socket and slid down the side, which I registered in slow motion. I glanced at it in the heat of the training, kept going, and then a moment later thought, *I must have mis-seen what I think I saw.* Turns out, no, I hadn't—it was mangled. The two joints were dislocated, and the top part of the finger had slid down inside the skin.

Needless to say, it takes a moment to process something like that.

I looked at my buddy Raymond Jordan, a teammate of mine from Mizzou who was sitting on the side of the mats, and said, "I need to go to the hospital; can you set it up for me?"

They took me to a hospital in Minsk, stitched me up, and put a cast on it. On our way back to the training camp, the translator asked me, "In America, how much does a procedure like this cost?" He meant the X-rays, the numbing of the arm, the stitches, the cast—all the treatment I'd just received.

I said, "I don't know, but I'm sure it would be very damn expensive."

He looked at me and—I'll never forget—said, "You know how much this costs here?" He allowed a moment for the drama to build. "Maybe we'll give him a bottle of wine or something..."

I was like, oh shit. I already had this sinking feeling that I didn't get the treatment I needed, which was doubly alarming with a fight coming up in four weeks. Knowing I needed my finger to heal exceedingly fast, I immediately called the airline and asked to get on the next available flight back to the States.

Good thing I did.

When I got back home the doctor took the cast off, re-X-rayed my finger and discovered that the doctor in Belarus—who I could only imagine was somewhere enjoying a nice bottle of Bordeaux—had stitched into a nerve in my finger.[50] The American doctor used a forceps to pull it out, and the pain shot all the way through my body. It was agony, like nothing I've ever felt in my life. Then he restitched it up and told me to be avoid using it.

The countdown was on to my Bellator debut.

That meant I had less than a month to heal, and I started calling myself the "one-handed bandit" in the short training camp. I couldn't use my damn right arm to train for my Bellator debut against Ryan Thomas. Of course, I didn't utter a peep of any of this to Bellator, because there was no way in hell I was going to miss my opportunity to fight on the bigger stage. I was competing even if they had to cut my finger off. To top it all off, I got married to Amy just six days before the fight.

Looking back on those early days in MMA, I can't help but wonder, how did I do all that? It wasn't very smart.

Thomas, a UFC veteran with a strong submission game who'd already faced guys like Matt Brown and Ben Saunders, would be my first real competition. The fight was held at the Chicago Theatre, and I showed up in gold and black trunks to represent Mizzou. Not being able to grip anything with my right hand, my whole goal for the bout was to not take any damage. Just don't get hit. Being that it was a tournament, and I stood to fight three times in nine weeks, I wanted to come out unscathed. Thomas called himself "The Tank Engine," but the plan was to outwork him, to outgrapple him, to break him,

---

50   I saved the X-ray for a long-ass time, as it was a great centerpiece to tell the story.

and most importantly, avoid taking any damage.

For the most part, it worked—though there was controversy. After taking him down in the first half minute, he cinched a triangle, which looked more dramatic than it was. I was able to pop out of there easily enough, and from there I controlled the action. I ended up with an arm-in guillotine choke that was in pretty tight, and the referee, after asking Thomas for a sign that he was okay and getting a limp nothing in response, stopped the fight. Thomas immediately argued that he didn't tap and, as evidenced by his lucid protest, was still very much conscious, but the fight was over. It went down as a "technical submission," and the crowd in Chicago didn't like it that Thomas (who was from Illinois) was shorted.

It sucked to win like that, but it was the ref's call. Right away, there was talk of a rematch. Thomas was all over the internet lobbying for one. I was cool with it. I didn't see how he would hurt me in a second encounter, so why not? And as luck would have it, a strange turn of events paved the way for Thomas to get the chance to avenge himself.[51] We fought less than a month later in Grand Prairie, Texas, an oil pump–lined suburb of Dallas. I wanted to finish him more definitively in the second fight, but instead I just dominated for fifteen minutes. He didn't have anything for me. That silenced Ryan Thomas and got me into the tournament finals.

Still harboring a less and less realistic thought of wrestling, I actually competed in the US World Team Finals on June 11 out in Iowa—just six days before the welterweight finale with Dan Hornbuckle in Bellator. At that point in time I felt I could spin plates and fight at the same time. The wrestling tournament didn't go particularly well. I didn't compete up to my standards, and I lost in the semifinals. I realized that it was

---

51 No lie, a fucking volcano in Iceland prevented Jim Wallhead from traveling over for his fight with Jacob McClintock, which opened the door for Thomas to step in and take his place. He beat McClintock easily to advance to a rematch with me in the semis. By the way, I only remember these names because I looked. I didn't know who they were at the time.

impossible to continue wrestling while doing MMA full time. It was really stupid, and I shouldn't have done it. My wrestling career was over.

Still, I resolved to let my wrestling continue dictating everything I did in the cage, session after session, at the Lion's Den in Scottsdale. Everyone would know that I came from the world of wrestling. My passion for it would just take on a modified form. I would show that wrestling was the best base in MMA.

The finale with Hornbuckle, at an outdoor venue in Kansas City, was the most hyped fight of my life to that point. They put together a video package on Hornbuckle, who was Native American from Cherokee, North Carolina, selling him somewhat as a sentimental favorite. As for me, I was expected to roll. Amy said I was "almost like a hippie" in the canned promo, which was amusing.

I wasn't about to try to appease a crowd looking for a certain aesthetic. My style was even more "funky" in MMA than it had been in those wild scrambling days on the college mats. My stand-up looked awkward (in large part because it was), which had one writer in the media comparing it to "watching a foal stand up for the first time after being born." The media was intrigued because I spoke my mind and I had the Olympic pedigree, the hair, the unapologetic, fuck-all attitude—refreshing things when promoting confrontations. I was marketable, even if a little raw. But I wasn't a striker because I didn't need to be. I was going to put people on their backs and make life miserable for them for as long as I had to.

The ground was my world, and everybody knew it.

That dogged pursuit to take people down rubbed some the wrong way. It opened eyes, too. I didn't have all the tools that seasoned MMA fighters had, but I had a strong suit that could trump all that "well-roundedness." To me, it was kind of funny to hear people talk about how they were going to beat me. Beat me how? From your back, while fending off elbows and punches?

That's how it went down against Hornbuckle, whom I beat handily over three rounds to win the Season Two tournament. I tortured him, just like I told everyone I would beforehand. I happily telegraphed my every intention and dared Hornbuckle to stop it. Within fifteen seconds he was on his back. I kept him there, more or less, the entire time. He would get up; I'd dump him down. He would try to cover up; I'd drop hammer-fists into his face. I wanted to finish him, and I tried, but I just didn't have all the tools yet. I had only begun competing sixteen months before. Still, the fight could have been 30–24 after the three rounds, but instead I was given a standard 30–27 unanimous decision. I won the tournament.

I made the $100,000 through three fights.

I told the crowd and the critics afterward that they shouldn't have doubted me. "Shame on you," I said. I was having fun. Now I would get a shot at the Bellator title, which at that time was held by Lyman Good.

Bjorn Rebney, who was Bellator's first CEO and the man in charge when I was there, was an interesting person. He had worked as a lawyer before getting into the fight game, and he had all the charm of a lawyer, which plenty of fight fans didn't connect with. Bellator's model of holding tournaments was always under scrutiny, and Bjorn just never seemed to endear himself with fans the way that Dana White did when Zuffa purchased the UFC in the early 2000s.

People generally hated him, but I got along with Bjorn for the most part; I never had too many issues with him. Though, I do remember one time he tried to pull a fast one on me, and I don't believe it was the first time he'd attempted it. My contract with Bellator was conditionally for nine fights, and he called me one day when I was on fight number eight against Karl Amoussou. I'd mentioned to him that I only had one fight left after Karl, and he said, "Oh, no, you have four fights left."

I said, "How do you figure?"

Well, Bjorn said, the original deal was six fights, and "if you won the tournament or the belt, it's three additional fights, so that's six total additional fights because you won both." I was like, *Bjorn, that's a load of bullshit, that's not what the contract says.* So I went back and looked at the original contract, and, sure enough, it said if you do any of these things it's three fights, not three fights per. He thought I'd be a sucker. That's how shitty MMA was in those days.[52] He thought he could just say something like that and I'd just shrug my shoulders and say, "Well, I guess I have three more fights."

Bellator as a promotion fell under a kind of dark cloud during the Bjorn years, which overlapped my years at Bellator the whole way. A lot of UFC-centric fans and media didn't pay any attention to it, and I think Bjorn might've appeared tone-deaf to some of the critics. For me, it was perfectly fine. I was learning on the fly, winning tournaments and making money.

Now I was getting a title shot against Bellator's first welterweight champion, Lyman Good. Some people tend to think that if you win a title in a national fight promotion— which Bellator was at the time, though still behind Strikeforce and light years behind the UFC—you get rich. That's not really true.

In fact, when I fought Good for the belt I actually got less money in purse than I had in the previous fight winning the tournament. My pay structure for the first three fights was $10,000 to show and $10,000 to win, then $15,000/$15,000 and $25,000/$25,000, adding up to a total of $100,000. For my first fight out of the tournament I made $14,000/$14,000,

---

52 All the way back in 2012, LOL!

even though it was for a title. Not that I was complaining. At that time I felt like $100,000 for the three fights was relatively good pay, considering my experience level. A step back didn't really bother me; it was still decent money.[53]

The other thing was that back then—circa 2010–2012—sponsorship money was really good. My management company, Zinkin, had a lot of connections in the industry, and I probably made at least as much money in sponsorships in those first fights as I did in purse. Companies like CageHero, Everlast, and Oak Grove were paying big money to have their brand strewn across my trunks. Fighters were visible and fighting was booming, so people were throwing money around all over the place, not realizing they would never get a return on their investments. When the sponsor dollars dried up, they dried up hard; but for a while there, I was in the tall clover, happily using myself as a human billboard when I fought.

On October 21, 2010, just a year and a half into my MMA career, I won my first title. I took it from Lyman Good, a Tiger Schulmann fighter from New York who'd won the first season's welterweight tournament and entered our fight with a perfect 10–0 record. It got super dicey at the end, and I absorbed the hardest strike I ever took in an MMA fight. I was having my way with Lyman all the way through until late in the fifth round, when, from a desperate position on his back as I dove into his guard, he landed an upkick from hell, which brought the fans in Philadelphia to their feet in the way that a Hail Mary in football might.

I collapsed after taking that kick and kind of auto-crawled back into him as he attempted a triangle, which, I'll admit, was really tight. I was out of it. When you're stunned you don't realize what's happening, and in my head I had slipped. That's the conclusion I came to when I discovered I was fighting my way

---

53 Nate Quarry always bitches that he only received $10,000 for his title fight with Rich Franklin at UFC 56, which was only a few years earlier. Comparatively I was doing okay.

out of a triangle; I had merely slipped, not taken a sole to the face. I got out of the triangle by stepping over and popping my head out. It wasn't until later when I watched back and understood all at once...holy shit, I got rocked there. That was a hard, hard shot. I never got dropped like that before, and I wouldn't get dropped like that again in any of my Bellator fights, which was a kind of unacknowledged paradox. For somebody who sucked on his feet, I almost never really got hit.

Lyman got me, but I was able to shake it off and win the fight, and I now had a belt around my waist. I was a champion.

I had been training with Alan Belcher, a tough UFC veteran famous for having this amazing tattoo of Johnny Cash down the biceps of his left arm. My side gig coaching at Arizona State wasn't working out the way I'd hoped. Besides, as the Bellator champion I was making three times more as a fighter than I was a coach, so I made the long-overdue decision to fight full time. No more wrestling, and no more college coaching.

After a non-title fight with Nick Thompson out in Newkirk, Oklahoma, in June,[54] which I dominated from the first seconds to the final horn, I decided to join Belcher back home in Milwaukee, at Duke Roufus's gym. It was at Duke's that I found my permanent home to train. He was a great kickboxing coach, and there was a roomful of veterans in there that all had areas they were strong in. Anthony Pettis was the WEC champion and was just getting rolling in the UFC, and he was known for his striking. There were others in there like Eric Koch and Alan and Anthony's younger brother Sergio, and, later, Gerald Meerschaert.

From the beginning, Duke was vigilant about defense, which fit into my style. In my first year and a half of MMA training I'd roll with guys like Jon Fitch and Jake Shields and

---

54   Which was an odd thing. Bellator wanted to stick with the thesis that you had to win a tournament before you could fight for a title, which wasn't a very functional way to go about things. Because nobody had won a tourney yet to qualify, they didn't want to leave me, the champion, on the bench forever waiting for that to happen.

realize, if I don't get knocked out no one can beat me.[55] I kept thinking, *I can outgrapple any of these dudes, no problem...just don't get clocked*. So, for that portion of my career, it was a heavy focus on defense, number one, and number two, I was figuring out how to penetrate the gap. That meant going from being in front of them to being on top of them before they could hit me.

As I was getting set to defend the title against Jay Hieron, that was the central focus of my training. It's something that most wrestlers screw up. A lot of times wrestlers will punch, kick, and then shoot and entirely miss the in-between. One of the absolutely instrumental things I did in sparring during five-round days was, instead of saying, okay, I'm going to take Gerald or Anthony down once and then I'm not going to keep them there the whole time, I would make myself average a takedown a minute. It was similar to how I operated in competition in high school, and it kept my focus on dominating. On the motor. On penetrating the gap, again and again.

So if I took them down and I held them for two minutes, I still needed to take them down four more times in that round. I'd have to let them up. If I failed to get five in that first round, and I only get four takedowns, in the next round I needed to get six. It has to average out to one a minute over twenty-five minutes. Being big into sports psychology, this was effective. I made it a point to always complete the goal. Essentially, what I was doing was penetrating the gap twenty-five times, which, in an actual fight, could overwhelm a striker.

Though I was now making good money, I still wasn't rich by a long shot. Coming from a blue-collar family, I'd never really been poor, and I was always pretty thrifty. I lived in a little house my parents had bought off campus, and with the money I'd made doing summer camps during all four summers

---

55 I also rolled jiu-jitsu with the Diaz brothers, Nick and Nate, and I always felt like they were kind of noodly—I could do whatever I wanted with them. Just some trivia thought you might like to know.

of my college career I paid for that house in full. I got a check for $700 every month in scholarship money from Mizzou and saved all of it. As a graduation present, my parents gave me a 2007 Prius, which I drove for the next decade. I definitely knew how to live lean.

It was a gradual build to make ends meet and save money along the way. In 2007, I made around $50,000, and the next year—2008, the year of the Olympics—something like $70,000. As I segued into MMA in 2009, my earnings went down considerably, but, because I'd saved that money, I felt rich compared to where my college friends were. I'd literally spent nothing, which was why my wife accused me of being the least materialistic person she knew in the video promo before my Hornbuckle fight.

Even in my brokest days, when I was beginning to generate money wrestling, I began stashing away $2,000 a month in a Northwestern Mutual Full Life Insurance policy long-term account. During my leanest years, this was extremely tough to swallow, but I've always been stubborn about what I set out to do. Remember, I gave up pizza and fast food and soda when I was in fifth grade to lose weight for long-term success in wrestling. I've been socking that money away since I was twenty-three, and in 2021—the year I am writing this—there is over $350,000 in that account.[56] That nest egg operated as a fallback for me. If I were to flunk out of fighting or run out of all my other money, I'd still have that.

Having a little money from my Bellator run allowed me to buy a house in Wisconsin. It was a modest two-bedroom that we bought for $170,000, and we had to borrow the down payment money from my mom. But I liked my earning potential, and the Hieron fight was to pay me $18,000/$18,000, so I knew I would be getting $36,000 soon.

The fight was held at the Memorial Hall in Kansas City, the same town in which I'd beaten Hornbuckle to win the initial tournament. Hieron was a tough UFC veteran

56 These days I invest heavily in crypto, so it's an evolved sacrifice.

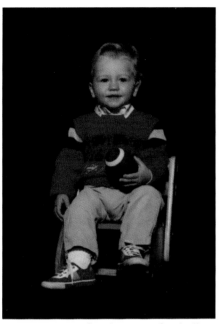

At age 2 my first love was football.

With my baby brother Max.

Honing my striking skills at age 3.

Chunky Ben loves baseball, 1994.

Working on my wrestling skills as a middle schooler, January 1998.

Learning to promote from an early age, 2001.

Flanked by my high school coach John Mesenbrink and future UFC champion Jonny Hendricks, ready to compete at Fargo with the best hair ever.

Completing a dream by winning the 2002 junior national championships. In third place is Jake Herbert, whom I'd later beat in the NCAA Finals in 2006. He would go on to be a world silver medalist in 2010.

I win my first national title, 2006.

Celebrating with Max after he won the national title, 2010.

One of my dreams upon going to the University of Missouri comes to fruition as Mizzou wins its first ever team trophy, 2007.

Celebrating pinning my first opponent at the 2008 Olympics.

2008 U.S. Men's Freestyle Olympic Wrestling Team

Left to right: Me, Henry Cejudo, Doug Schwab, Daniel Cormier, Steve Mocco, and Andy Hrovat

Winning the Bellator title against
Lyman Good.

Lather, rinse, repeat.
This time against Karl Amoussou.

Douglas Lima was a beast but I beat him across the board,
50-45 on all three scorecards.

Defending the Bellator title for the first time against Jay Hieron.

Hammering Shinya Aoki in my (first) retirement fight at ONE Championship.

*Even though Dana refused to sign me in 2013,
things with the UFC worked out in 2019.*

*Me with my wonderful family—my wife Amy,
and my kids Alex, Andi and Ozi, with our dog, Gaia.*

who'd fought Georges St-Pierre back in the day and was on a ten-fight win streak. Experience-wise, he had twenty-six pro fights to my eight. Once again I got off to a slow start, and Jay was able to stuff some of my takedown attempts in the first round. But through the middle rounds I controlled the action, taking him down and having my way with him. In the fifth round he landed a spinning back kick that landed in my chest, which excited the crowd a little bit. But he bookended two decent rounds against my three dominant ones, and—though he didn't like it one bit, and made it known to anyone who would listen—I won a split decision.

When I won the Jay Hieron fight, I paid my mom back for the down payment on the house. It was during that time, in 2011, that I also opened up the Askren Wrestling Academy (AWA) in Hartland. I was rolling along pretty well, but there was this "boring" accusation that I kept dealing with, as in, Askren is boring to watch. Askren doesn't finish anybody. Askren's style is insufferable, his stand-up stinks, and when he gets the fight where he wants it—which is on the ground—it devolves into a snoozefest.

I took all of that in stride. Some might even say I took it "smugly," which I did. I knew my submission skills and ground-and-pound were coming along, and besides, I was being held to a different standard than most fighters of my experience level. I fought pretty immediately after wrestling in 2009, and then just a year and a half later I was fighting in a Bellator tournament (and winning it), before fighting for a Bellator belt (and winning that too). Because I'd won the Bellator title less than two years into my career, people viewed me as a guy who's been in the sport a long time, a guy who's been a champion for a while.

Only I hadn't. Things were happening for me at warp speed.

I was a fighter who didn't have a lot of skills outside of wrestling, yet I was thrust into winning at a high level and was forced to learn on the fly. I had a stretch early on where

I won decisions, which took on patterns of dominance with virtually no real threat of a finish. I understood why that can be frustrating to fans. People got mad because they thought my next fight with the highly ranked Douglas Lima in April 2012 was really good, but—though I dominated him for twenty-five minutes—I couldn't seem to hurt him or really even come close to submitting him. I dominated without the threat of a finish, which to some—especially Lima himself—meant a twenty-five-minute sentence.

Lima was tough, though. He had just beaten Ben Saunders to win the latest welterweight tournament and was quietly great. Though I got a clean sweep of the score-cards—50–45 on all three—I just didn't have the full set of tools to make him stop. The fact that I dominated him in a way he'd never been dominated (and never would be again) should have been the larger story, but with a media fixed on established narratives, my inability to finish a fight was talked about more.

I was getting closer, though. I was learning to use my elbows more effectively, to smash the intended targets on the ground. It took me a minute, but my time at Roufusport was paying off. I started figuring things out.

I showed that when I fought the Frenchman Karl Amoussou out in Thackerville, Oklahoma, in early 2013. The Amoussou fight was the first time I truly unleashed hell on an opponent. The doctors called the fight off after three rounds because I'd opened up a crevasse on his head. He needed something like thirty-seven stitches because of all the elbows I slammed into him. The elbows were now a huge weapon for me.

Was that boring? I didn't give a shit either way. I was loving it.

If that didn't change the perception, the next fight against Andrey Koreshkov did. I fought the Russian Koreshkov in Rio Grande, New Mexico, but when I was done with him he might've thought he'd been abducted and dropped off in Roswell. I hit Koreshkov 248 times over eighteen minutes, outstriking him officially 248–3. Realistically, I can recall him hitting me just once. Only one strike of his actually landed. I abused him so badly and came very close to submitting him a couple of times and absorbed no punishment whatsoever.

The idea was to dominate fights, to get the finish if I could, but to take as little damage as possible. Boring?

Part of that "boring" thing was perpetuated by the UFC's Dana White. He tweeted out that he'd "rather watch flies fuck" than watch me fight and that "Ambien took Ben Askren to sleep." He planted those "boring" seeds on Twitter, and a large segment of MMA fans took what Dana said as gospel, without forming their own opinions. He was the catalyst for the early established opinion on my stand-up. That was in 2012, right after I'd called him a liar on some stuff he said about PEDs (more on that momentarily). It was also right in the midst of my non-finish streak, which made me an easy target for his retaliations. I didn't lose a round between Thomas, Horn-buckle, Good, and Thompson, but because I didn't finish any of them he took his shot.

By the time I routed Koreshkov, I knew I wasn't boring—I was an existential nightmare. An acquired taste. A dictator of wills. People could call it whatever they wanted, but you knew how a fight with me would go beforehand, without variation. I was so dominant at what I wanted to do that it came off as transparent and telegraphed; it followed frustrating patterns of predictability. People hate the concept of "inevitable" in fighting, but I brought it roaring to life. I was a wrestler with wrestling roots, and I dared you to stop it. Nobody could. I wrestled unapologetically. I was going to showcase wrestling in all its superiority.

Wrestling to me was life.

Better yet (or worse, depending on your vantage point), I wasn't taking any damage. Each fight was strictly one-way traffic. The Hieron, Lima, and Amassou fights told the story. Those three were some of the most high-powered guys in the world. I fought thirteen rounds with them combined, and not one of them could land any kind of hard shot with me. Not one.

Every fight starts on the feet, and through sixty-five minutes of cagetime they couldn't touch me. Koreshkov landed a single strike and absorbed 248. So how bad was my stand-up? A big part of the game—and having longevity—is not to take damage.

It depended on the lens in which you chose to view it.

People would cling to their early perceptions of the "funky" wrestler with subpar-to-downright-awful striking who couldn't put people out of their misery, and those perceptions would stick with me for the rest of my career...even if eleven of my final twelve fights ended in finishes.

And as I knew I was ready to cash in in a bigger way, it turned out that most of those finishes would take place outside of Bellator. My fight with Koreshkov was the final fight on my contract. I went 9–0 in Bellator, while establishing myself as a polarizing figure in MMA and a reigning, undefeated champion.

Now I was a free agent.

CHAPTER SIX:
UFC

"I have a friend that told me my power was my influence and I said, 'My power is to not be influenced.'"

—Kanye West

Everyone was wondering if I was headed to the UFC, which made the most logical sense. That's where "the best fighters in the world" were, as Dana White was so fond of telling everyone. In the previous months, Bellator had lost a couple of its free-agent champions to the UFC, including Héctor Lombard and lightweight champ Eddie Alvarez—and both situations were a little messy. With Héctor, the UFC was forced to overpay to dissuade Bellator from matching, and numbers were revealed to the public.

When Eddie signed with the UFC during his own free agency, Bellator exercised that same "matching" clause in his contract after the period of exclusive negotiation, which kicked up a shitstorm. Settlement meetings were held. Eddie got vocal in the media about the situation. Veteran fighters, seeing the money he was being offered from the UFC (not to mention the pay-per-view points), got pissed off. Eddie got sued by Bellator and found himself not only caught in a contract dispute, but ultimately back with the promotion. Begrudgingly he had to return for two more fights, which ended up being one.[57] It made for a lot of bad feelings between fans and Bellator.

I didn't want any of that to happen. Neither did Bellator or the UFC, which hated when information on fighter pay became public. The matching clause was a problem that I needed to figure out before doing anything.

In truth, I genuinely *believed* I was headed to the UFC. At this point, I was undefeated, a perfect 12–0, vocal, polarizing, dismissive of certain media,[58] smug, confident, cocky, and all kinds of other adjectives that got thrown around in the media. That I was a dominant champion was all that truly mattered. Yet I was also disinterested in kowtowing to promoters who tried to govern and control fighters. I needed to be who I was, and I wasn't going to let Dana White or anybody change that. I've never cared for liars, which is tough because the best liars in the sport are the ones at the top.

I had already poked the bear a fair amount by the time I reached free agency in the summer of 2013. I'd called Dana White a fat, bald liar (or something to that effect) on Twitter, and—for a guy so often accused of not having any stand-up—I never pulled any punches with my opinions.

Dana didn't care for me, but there was a bit of foreshadowing involved, too, which I really had nothing (everything) to do with.[59] The MMA site Sherdog had put out a feature article about me as a prospect around 2009, which ran right in the heart of fight week for a UFC event. Dana saw that and, for some petty reason, lost his mind. *The audacity of an MMA site running an article that had nothing to do with*

---

57 Once Scott Coker took over for Bjorn Rebney as the president of Bellator, one of the first things he did to win over fans was release Eddie Alvarez, allowing him to sign with the UFC.

58 Namely Ariel Helwani, with whom I had beef for talking shit about my fight with Douglas Lima. He "banned" me from his show. I tweeted to him that I didn't want to discuss the merits of my style with a non-fighter, while inviting him "to go in a cage with me—when you do that I'll do your show. Otherwise kiss my ass." We later reconciled.

59 Everything?

his upcoming event! Dana believed that all coverage should center around what mattered in the world of fighting: that is, whatever *he* was doing.

He turned bright red. He complained that the idiots over at Sherdog were running some story about this curly-headed wrestler guy rather than the UFC card he was promoting. I caught my first glimpse of what it's like to receive backlash from Dana fans, and I hadn't done anything other than coexist. I guess a media site splitting coverage between us was enough to start a strong (if inadvertent) vendetta against me. I didn't realize it at the time, but right then and there—without doing a damn thing wrong—we were off on the wrong foot.

It didn't help matters that I regularly called him out for his bullshit in subsequent years. Especially on the USADA front in 2012.

Dana had said in the media that testing his roster of athletes for illegal substances and PEDs would be impossible, and I merely pointed out, ever so delicately, that this wasn't true. What I actually tweeted was, "The USOC random tests Olympic athletes in all sports. Dana saying testing his fighters would be impossible is a bald-faced lie." Two hours after I posted that, Dana responded with his instantly famous riposte to a fan who was provoking him by showing him my tweet: "When Ambien can't sleep it takes Ben Askren. The most boring fighter in MMA history. I would rather watch flys (*sic*) fuck."

In truth, I found myself a little regretful for having called him out. Dana's the type to hold grudges until his knuckles turn white, but when I said that, I was still a year or so away from free agency, plenty of time (I assumed) to let bygones be bygones. Never mind that I was ultimately right—the UFC brought on the third-party United States Anti-Doping Agency to regularly (and randomly) test its entire roster in 2015—I had made Dana's permanent shit list. I saw it as a calculated risk. Dana cares about money more than anything in the world, so I had it in the back of my head that, as long as I could make Dana money, he'd forgive any inconsequential social media skirmishes.

As it turned out, that was a miscalculation.

The grudge was alive and well in 2013, and it traced back to somewhere...the idea that I personally usurped coverage of an event, a bad ratio on insubordination to reverence for what he'd done and who he was, the USADA thing...only Dana really knows. But I saw just how much he had it in for me that summer, when I was finally eligible to sign on with the UFC.

Behind the scenes, the UFC was telling me they were interested. It was mostly Lorenzo Fertitta, the owner of Zuffa, sending those signals. Lorenzo was making it clear that the UFC wanted me, but the only sticking point was that he didn't want to deal with the matching issue, recalling what had just happened with Hector and Eddie. The indications I got were that if we could work around the matching clause, the UFC would take care of the rest.

There was a big pay-per-view event coming up less than a month after my final fight with Bellator, which was UFC 164 in my hometown of Milwaukee. The back-and-forth heated up because naturally that would've been a great card to have me on, even with the time crunch. So I called Bjorn at Bellator to see about facilitating my release.

Bellator was interested in re-signing me, but the truth of the matter was they didn't want to re-sign me *that* bad. They offered a little bit more than I'd been making, which in the end was negligible, so I told Bjorn outright that I wouldn't be coming back and asked him to release me.[60] The timing

---

60 Not that Bjorn didn't see it all coming. Looking back on my career in Bellator, I didn't fully understand the business of it all, really. I was on the cover of *FIGHT! Magazine* in 2012, accompanying a feature written by Chuck Mindenhall. In the piece I said something to the effect that going to the UFC was *inevitable* to me, and Bjorn fucking lost his mind. I probably shouldn't have said that. Bellator didn't want to be seen as the minor leagues to the UFC or some kind of stepping-stone, and I didn't fully get it. I was just being truthful. I wanted to fight the best guys, so to me it did seem like an inevitability.

was right, and there was precedent. I reminded him of the bad publicity Bellator received over the Eddie issue, when Bellator retained him in that legal battle and came off as the bad guys in the scenario, like the ultimate blockers of fun. Nobody wanted a repeat of that.

I can remember how it all went down to this day because my wife and I made *tom kha gai* soup that night, and we had to go out to get the ingredients. It was a Thursday night, and Bjorn called me up and said, "Okay, we're going to give you a full, outright release, under two conditions. Number one, you don't say anything bad about Bellator. Keep it classy. And two, you don't announce it before we do. It must come from Bellator first."

I agreed, assuming that we were doing away with any roadblocks to a UFC deal. Now that things were heating up, Dana had publicly changed his tune almost entirely by then. He'd been telling the press for the last few weeks, "We want Ben Askren, yes, we want to sign Ben Askren." Things were setting up nicely to bury the hatchet and work together.

The plan was for Bellator to announce my release on Monday, meaning I'd have to stay mum for the weekend. I signed the paperwork, sent it off that night, and then faxed it to UFC headquarters first thing Friday morning, alerting UFC officials that we were good to go. I felt fine about things, but then on Friday afternoon in Toronto—during one of the old fight week scrums he used to do at big events, which I happened to be watching from my house—Dana inexplicably reversed course.

When somebody asked if there was any movement on striking a deal with me, he said, "We have no interest in Ben Askren."

No interest? I sat there stunned, thinking...*Wait, what the hell just happened? For weeks now you've been saying we want Ben Askren publicly, and now I'm sitting on the couch, with the knowledge that I literally just faxed the UFC my release paperwork, which I wasn't able to say anything about, and here you are going on record saying you have no interest?* I called my agent and said, "Fly me to UFC head-quarters in Vegas and we'll get to the bottom of it."

Daniel Cormier, who had the same representation as I did, came along on the trip, too. UFC 165 had just taken place that weekend in Toronto, which is where the classic light heavyweight title fight between Alexander Gustafsson and Jon Jones took place, so Cormier was in the wings to challenge Jones next.

Looking back on the meeting, I wish I'd been more bold. In my head I thought Dana—a businessman who gets what he wants—would fuck around a little bit and then say, "Okay, it's a done deal." But I ended up speaking to Lorenzo in person that day, with Dana patching through on the little speaker phone from Toronto. I thought the conversation went well enough, and later that day the UFC came back with a peculiar offer.

They said it would be a confidential contract, and they wanted me to fight one fight in the World Series of Fighting (WSOF) before coming over, saying that Zuffa would pay for the whole thing. A one-off fight with the WSOF?

I said exactly what flashed through my head. "That's really fucking stupid and bizarre, and people will see through it."[61] It *was* stupid. Yet I also let them know that, if this was what they wanted, I was more than willing to play the game to get into the UFC. I said I'd be willing to do a fight in WSOF. I just assumed there was something in WSOF's inclusion that we didn't fully understand, but if that was the simplest way to strike a deal I was all for it.

Satisfied with the situation, I went back to my hotel to pack, and just before I boarded my plane to fly back to Wisconsin, I received a sobering call from my agent. The UFC had pulled the offer. No revised offer was forthcoming. No explanation was

---

61 I'm no good at softening my thoughts in moments like that, and I am unable to lie. So I can sound short, but really I am just being transparent and clear on my opinion.

given. When I asked if we could jump on a quick call so they could make sense of the bait-and-switch, they wouldn't even do that. The deal was dead, stillborn, and I was given no official reason for it.

Just *pffft*, gone.

I DMed Lorenzo. "Hey, I don't want to be rude. I worked really hard to get the release from Bellator and came all the way to Vegas. Any way I can get one solid reason there is suddenly no interest?"

Nothing. Silence. Zilch.

The whole thing stung. I really believed I was UFC bound, and I think fans did too. I was in my prime and ready for the Johny Hendrickses and the Carlos Condits and the GSPs—all the guys who were part of the exclusive club. That sucked. Once again I was on the outside looking in. But, as always, there was no sense in dwelling on it. The only direction for me had to be forward.

I'd visited Singapore the year prior, right after my fight with Douglas Lima, to do a seminar at Evolve MMA and pick up some cash. During that trip I got the chance to spend time with ONE Championship founder Chatri Sityodtong, who also ran Evolve MMA, and Rich Franklin, the former UFC middleweight champion who was training for a fight with Wanderlei Silva at Evolve. We went out to dinner each night of my visit, and they told me a little bit about the promotion they were running. By the end of that trip I felt I knew Chatri fairly well, and I found that I really enjoyed him as a person. He was a straight shooter.

So, that night, after getting spurned by the UFC, I texted Chatri: "Have any interest in a welterweight? Maybe a one-year deal or something?" From across the globe he came back immediately with, "Why not a two-year deal?" And I said, just as simply, "Yeah, you know what, fuck the UFC, why not a two-year deal?"

Boom. It was that easy. When one door closes another one opens, or whatever the hell that old saying is.

It wasn't as though I didn't have other options. Immediately after the UFC's strange detour plan for me fell through, WSOF got in touch independently to see if they might sign me outright. They were giving off such a strange, disingenuous vibe that I didn't particularly like. They were so subservient that it was instantly off-putting. I could tell something was up.

Looking back, I think the UFC had told them, "Hey, Askren has no other options, go sign him," thinking I was desperate (and gullible) with no real leverage. To their credit, they shot their shot, but their offers felt flimsier than a house of cards.

I took a group of kids somewhere on a wrestling tournament that week, and Ali Abdelaziz—the fight manager at Dominance—and other WSOF owners would not stop calling. I told them, "I can't talk business right now, I'm on a bus with a group of kids." They kept calling anyway. And calling. *And calling.* And they kept changing the offers with each call, as if whatever whimsical idea popped in their head had to be discussed immediately. "How about $50K/$50K?" they'd say. Then next time, "How about $80,000 flat?" I'd be like, well, that's less than $50K/$50K, isn't it? Then they'd call back, "How about an advertisement on a ring post?"

It was random, weird stuff, over and over. That turned me off. I figured the WSOF must be in serious financial trouble, which ended up being the case. Still, I understood. Why wouldn't the WSOF assume I was up shit creek without a paddle? I'd burned the bridges with Bellator, and now the UFC had slammed the door on me, so where was I going to go? They were operating under the notion that I was screwed. I wasn't.

I'd made up my mind to go to Asia, to win another title with ONE Championship. Finding another option when Dana was trying to force me to the WSOF felt not only good but right. I wasn't going to be bullied into some direction by the UFC, because I had already resolved that I'd be content with my career if I never stepped foot in the Octagon. Besides, Amy and I liked to travel. We'd been to Singapore and were interested in touring other ports of Asia. Why shouldn't the next chapter of my career carry some adventure? As far as silver linings go, this was a good one.

All these years later, I'd still like to sit down with Dana and ask him why it didn't work the first time through, when I was ready to join ranks in the prime of my career. With me being a top name in the sport—a name that fans knew and cared about—why did he make my free agency period such a strange, irresolute experience? Why the sudden cold feet?

When I reflect on it, I think some of it had to do with me being so affiliated with the Bellator brand that there was a fear I could actually win a title in the UFC and inadvertently give merit to Bellator, who'd grown me from college athlete to MMA champion. Bellator could say, "Look, our guy became a champion over there." I imagine there was a fear of me debunking the notion that the best fighters are in the UFC.[62]

I think it was in December 2013 that I officially made my commitment to ONE Championship, signing a seven-fight deal. What I liked was that they were raring for me to go. They brought me over to do a weeklong press tour, with stops in Manila, Cambodia, Malaysia, Singapore, and Indonesia—a lot of foreign places that I'd never been to. The reception was awesome, and the enthusiasm with which they were promoting me felt good.

Better yet, they circled May for my first fight, which would be held in ONE's hub country of Singapore. I would take on Bakhtiyar Abbasov, a bronze medalist in Russian sambo who had a decent record of 11–2 at the time. The card was held at the Singapore Indoor Stadium in Kallang, a cone-shaped structure that held over ten thousand fans. It was a cool first experience.

Abbasov came out aggressive. He double-legged me in the first round, which I reversed within about five seconds. From there I pummeled him and punched him in the head a bunch of times, before sinking an arm triangle that choked him out. That was an easy night. After that fight I went to

---

62   One day, I hope Dana will open up with me about what went down.

Bali for a week with some friends who came over to see me, and it turned into a great trip. I wasn't in the UFC, but I was surrounded by beaches with turquoise water with tree-lined volcanic mountains in the mist.

I definitely wasn't bummed over how things were playing out. And I was just getting started.

Given that I was a star attraction for the promotion and a reigning champion from Bellator, ONE didn't waste any time giving me a title shot. In August, I went to Dubai for a welterweight title shot against Nobutatsu Suzuki, which lasted all of eighty-four seconds. Truth be told, there just wasn't much resistance. I took Suzuki down and put it on him and took zero damage for my efforts. That night, which was billed as ONE Championship 19: Reign of Champions, had three title fights in a row, including Shinya Aoki, who beat Kamal Shalorus to defend the lightweight title.

That night in far-off Dubai was memorable. There was a big time difference over there, and we were staying up all night to do the fight in the morning. I remember Dana White tweeted out something like, "Oh, we'd love to talk to Ben Askren now." I couldn't help but harass him and wrote back, "Oh thank you master @danawhite can I please have a shot?" At that point I was defiant. I felt like, go fuck yourself, you had the opportunity and you blew it.

Still, there was some vindication as far as the public was concerned, and now I was a champion again. I was staying busy, too, which was exactly the way I liked it.

But. Then. Things. Slowed. *Waaaay.* Down.

I suddenly found myself dealing with unwanted downtime, and I made the most of it helping my teammates. I was in Vegas in December to corner Anthony for his fight with Gilbert Melendez, which was a big weekend. Anthony was introduced as the latest star athlete to appear on the Wheaties box, and my old rival Johny Hendricks was in town to take on Robbie Lawler. That was also the weekend that the UFC announced that they were signing pro wrestling's CM Punk to a contract.

All I could think was, *What a joke.* So hypocritical.

I had booked myself on a red-eye to go back home after the fight card, and as I was sitting there at the airport, I was thinking about CM Punk (real name Phil Brooks) getting in the UFC despite having no actual experience to speak of. All he had for credentials were a celebrity name and an eager attitude. This made me reflect on all the silly bullshit I'd heard over the years.

Dana had mentioned on more than one occasion that I wasn't ready for the UFC because of my relative lack of experience, which made this signing of CM Punk laughable. So, I began firing shots, tweeting about it, while at the same time harassing Lorenzo Fertitta via his DMs.

"I understand you signed a fake wrestler for publicity reasons, but when you want a real one to come get that belt let me know," I wrote him. And just for good measure, I tossed in a jab at Johny Hendricks. "You can't want Hendricks as your champion, he is too dumb to draw in any fans attention."

Lorenzo didn't take the bait. He didn't reply.

Then things got interesting really quickly, and I changed my stance a bit. The next day I was in the gym and Duke told me, "Hey, Punk's coming to train with us here in Milwaukee." Just like that, Phil was a teammate. To his credit, he worked hard when he arrived. He was a good dude. He just wasn't that great at MMA. He wasn't very athletic, didn't move well, and didn't specialize in any one area. I appreciated him giving it a shot and all the hustle he showed, but it was apparent to me things wouldn't end well for him.[63]

Meanwhile, I had to wait until the following spring, April 2015, before my first title defense, which would come against Luís "Sapo" Santos out in Manila. I was a Muhammad Ali fan growing up, so fighting in Manila—the place where Ali and Joe Frazier finished their trilogy in 1975—was a cool correlation.

---

63 Phil went 0-2 in the UFC, and neither fight was competitive. A few years later he returned to pro wrestling.

Needless to say, Ali's fight was a lot more memorable than the one I had against Sapo.

They *said* Santos had a good first couple of minutes in our fight, meaning he kicked my legs a few times and stopped a couple of initial takedowns. I guess when people are so used to watching you dominate fights, any modicum of success stands out. Realistically, Santos was gassing big time just two minutes in when he pulled a stunt to get out of the fight. As I shot in around that mark and dumped him on the canvas he alleged I poked him in the eye, which, even now, I don't think I did. Worse, he declared himself unable to continue with the fight. Talk about a grand waste of time.

The fight was deemed a "no contest," and because people thought Sapo was competitive in the 120 seconds he lasted in there with me, the talks of a rematch kicked up. The fiasco stretched on into the fall as we tried to set up a second fight. The soonest they could make it was October or November, which meant I'd have a full six months to live with a fight that didn't go down on the official record. Doing a sequel to a nonexistent fight wasn't ideal. When we finally got it rescheduled for November, we traipsed all the way to the other side of the globe again—this time, back to Singapore—only to see Santos show up overweight. He missed weight by close to six pounds. To make things work, my only stipulation was for Sapo to weigh under 190 by the next day, something very lenient and doable to salvage the fight.

Santos said it wasn't possible. "I can't make it—I don't want to fight," he said.

He even went through a range of theatrics to ratchet up the drama, going to the hospital and carrying on that he was sick. It was all bullshit. That pissed me off. My whole year was wasted on Luís Santos, who couldn't work through a (bogus) eye-poke in our first fight and then couldn't make weight on his mulligan. There's nothing I hate more than spinning my wheels.

It would end up being an entire year between the first Santos fight and my next one, which occurred once again in Manila in April 2016. I would be fighting a big, jacked-up Russian by the name of Nikolay Aleksakhin. I had already been training at various gyms by this time, as I didn't get along with Duke's regular jiu-jitsu guy,[64] to the point that the only thing that I did at Roufusport in Milwaukee was spar twice a week. Yet on the long flight back over the Pacific, I watched the movie *Concussion* starring Will Smith, and it resonated with me to the point that I had an epiphany.

It occurred to me that I shouldn't be sparring at all.

For some people, fighting is all they've got. For me, I had a full life planned for after my MMA career, with my AWA gyms going full swing. What sense did it make to cause myself brain damage in the gym in preparation for a fight where real, concussive blows can be dealt? I'd been very good at minimizing damage in actual fights to that point, so why was I absorbing unnecessary blows in training? I resolved right then and there to give up sparring once and for all.

But first, I had to deal with Aleksakhin.

Of course, as if to tease my existentially draining dry run in which I had just one fight in two years, Aleksakhin missed weight. That meant my first official title defense would be rendered a non-title fight, another bummer. At least this time the fight was still on. I took it to Aleksakhin over the course of twenty-five minutes, taking a one-sided decision. I didn't take any real damage, either, which was the plan.

Since I was living in Wauwatosa, I'd been training at Duke's because of the proximity. When I got back I asked if I could rent the mat space when not in use, so I could bring in Gerald Meerschaert and Mike "Biggie" Rhodes to do mitts and drill sparring rather than having us try to kill each other during sessions. The new methods suited me just fine, but my hardships in keeping busy with fights continued.

---

64 I won't mention him by name, but he's a douche.

I signed an agreement to take on another Russian, this time by the name of Vitaly Bigdash, who was fighting out of Rostov-on-Don. The fight was scheduled to take place in Thailand, and given the exotic location, I saw it as a chance to parlay another vacation into the trip with some friends. We made plans to spend a week traveling around the country sightseeing after the fight, which was slated to take place in November.

Yet—once a-fucking-gain—it wasn't to be.

The king of Thailand, Bhumibol Adulyadej, passed away that October at the age of eighty-eight, which meant all activities in the country were cancelled. Thailand was essentially shut down, and so was my fight. After the yearlong episode with Sapo, this was a hard blow to absorb. There's nothing worse than being forced to idle when you're ready to fight, particularly when you're as impatient as I am.

Fortunately, my luck was about to change, and in 2017 things got back on track a little bit. I took on a Malaysian fighter named Agilan Thani in late May of that year back in Singapore. I won relatively easily by first-round submission. That same night on the card, Zebaztian Kadestam scored a TKO victory over Sapo, which set up a fight between Kadestam and me three and a half months later in Shanghai. Once again I was able to dominate the action, winning this time by a second-round TKO.

With two victories in a span of less than four months, signing on to fight Shinya Aoki, a huge name in Japan who was coming up from lightweight to challenge me, for my ONE Championship swan-song fight in November felt perfect. After such a long, frustrating inactive period, I would get three fights in six months, which was my kind of pace.

Aoki, as a drastically smaller fighter, didn't present much of a threat to me. I handled him in less than a minute, pounding him out with ground-and-pound, running my record to a perfect 18–0–(1).[65] Through those three fights in 2017, I never

---

65 Fucking Sapo.

got hit once. Not one solid blow. I couldn't have scripted it better; I came out of each fight in the same condition I'd arrived.

Throughout the year, I'd given it plenty of thought. My hips were deteriorating, and the writing was on the wall. I didn't want to keep fighting guys everyone knew I should (and would) beat. I wanted to fight the guys who so many people assumed I couldn't—the guys in the UFC, over there on the other side of the partition. I wanted to fight the very best in the world. I wanted them to fight *me*.

If that couldn't happen, after winning the Hodge twice in college and two world titles in MMA, I was perfectly content calling it a career. I'd done everything I wanted to do in combat, except for prove I was the best in the world. I vacated my ONE Championship title and retired from fighting with total sincerity, with the caveat in place that opened this book.

There was one little void left to fill.

I was either done or I was going to get the chance to prove I was the best in the world. No more detours. Then the trade happened, my retirement became a fight-game cliché by its sheer brevity, and everything changed quickly.

One of the rewarding things about finally arriving in the UFC—and specifically fighting at UFC 235 in March 2018 in Vegas, which featured title fights between Jon Jones and Anthony Smith, as well as Tyron Woodley against Marty Usman—was all the added media attention it garnered. My fight with Lawler was being dubbed the unofficial main event. Better yet, Dana had to promote a Ben Askren fight after years of bashing me as boring.

That was gratifying.

After a full decade of answering questions about me in the media and pretending I wasn't good enough and condemning my style, he was now in the position of having to promote me as something to behold. I found it hilarious, and I enjoyed the hell out of making my thoughts on the matter known.

I was the media focus that week, dominating the head-lines. Other welterweights were asked about me ad nauseam. Even with light heavyweight champ Jon Jones on the card, outlets were sending writers out specifically to cover me finally breaking the barrier to fight in the UFC. The Ringer sent Chuck Mindenhall out to do a big piece about my debut, and ESPN MMA did a poll asking if my fight was the unofficial main event. Even though my fight with Robbie was the swing bout on the pay-per-view, I won in a landslide—something like 70 percent voted it was the main attraction.

Of course, I was there to egg things on the whole way. I didn't hold back from telling the media that Dana didn't like me, and a big part of the allure that whole week was held taut on that line of tension between me and Dana. I made Dana uncomfortable by bringing up the feud during the press conference, and he did his best to downplay things. A major part of the buzz was how Dana had to essentially eat crow by acknowledging my very presence alongside him on the dais. It wasn't just me enjoying the moment; it was the media who'd long been onto Dana's tactics.

And it was tremendous to stop and consider just how intertwined my path had been with his through all the years. I realize a lot of fighters can make that claim because he's the president of the UFC, but it's made all the more remark-able that we'd never had—and still *have never had*—a real conversation, not even through texts. Some fighters talk about sitting down with Dana for a heart-to-heart and that kind of bullshit, but with me it was always a short, perfunc-tory transaction, just basic hellos. The only gesture the UFC ever extended to make amends for all those years of casting me as a pariah was offering to buy me a suit. A freaking *suit*.

Hunter Campbell told me that Dana wanted to buy me a suit when I was in Vegas, which apparently was his way of demonstrating that he didn't have it in for me. *I really like you; let me buy you a suit.* Never mind that I don't wear suits, that my entire wardrobe is almost exclusively T-shirts, shorts, and sandals; they wanted to make amends with the offering. I gave them a polite, "No thanks." Until Dana was ready to man up and talk to me, as far as I was concerned they could keep their hollow gestures.

In the back of my mind I knew the score, though. I had to strike hard in the UFC, make my run count, because at the most—being optimistic—I knew I might have eighteen months left to compete. My hips were near shot. The bone spurs were taking a toll. The pain was becoming less and less manageable. I had to keep revising my training based on how much my body would permit. If I was going to win a third title in the last major organization left on my list, I needed to do it quickly.

By now I knew how to promote myself. I'd had good experience in Bellator and ONE, and I was drawn to the guys who did it effectively as well as the guys who didn't. People like Leon Edwards were out there believing they were dealing in some kind of faithful meritocracy, and that simply wasn't how it worked in prizefighting. As mentioned before, it's not smart to look past an opponent literally, but it is wise to have the big picture in mind and plot your moves.

The most eyes are on you during that little window of time, the four days before your fight and the three days after. Every fighter should ask, how do I most effectively use that time? That's where the chance to manipulate the game takes place, to bend things to your will, plant seeds, kick up rivalries, manipulate headlines, piss off promoters, whatever. That's when everybody cares about your career the most.

I think everyone was feeling what I felt. My arrival to the UFC was a breath of fresh air for the entire welterweight division. I gave everyone extra juice because I was picking on all of them at once, and the media loves to make hypothetical fights. They love feuds. They love bad blood and disrespect and backstories. So much of the fight game is based on anticipation. I was picking on Usman, who was about to take on Tyron for the title. In fact, I was the reason people called him Marty, which he was known as in college. Once I started calling him that, a lot of people jumped on the bandwagon. I was picking on Colby Covington, a polarizing idiot that fans loved to hate, and he got some shine from that. I dismissed him altogether, saying he should just be expunged from the UFC. I wasn't shy about Jorge Masvidal, either, or Darren Till or anyone else.

Everyone benefitted from my arrival.

And it all started with Robbie.

Lawler wasn't a shell of himself when we met, but he wasn't the same "Ruthless" Robbie Lawler who had caved in Rory MacDonald's face at UFC 189, or the one who had butchered Johny Hendricks for five rounds, or the one who had put Carlos Condit through hell in another title defense. He had a reputation for shortening fighters' careers, which lent him a dangerous air to the media covering him. They thought I was actively provoking a killer and therefore inviting disaster. As I poked the bear all week long, laughing and having fun, Robbie remained shark-eyed and cold, which was perfect. If I was going to get my comeuppance, the No. 6–ranked Robbie was the right kind of dealer.

During the weigh-ins, people made a big deal of the fact that I spurned Dana White when he went to shake my hand. There I was, denying him the chance at reconciliation, thwarting the peace offering. The funny thing was that that was completely unintentional. I didn't even see him offer me a handshake (it didn't occur to me that he would do that!), and I chalked it up to my own "social cluelessness" when asked about it after the fight.

Before the fight, though, the media ate it up.

And now there was only one thing left to do.

Go out and fight.

Though I've made the walk thousands of times in different competitions, walking out for that fight was memorable because it was in the UFC. At thirty-four years old, entering the highly-anticipated last act of my career, here I was, at T-Mobile Arena in Las Vegas, hearing the opening of my walkout song "We Want the Funk" by Parliament hit the sound system. That song had accompanied me from the college mats to foreign lands, from Bellator to ONE, and finally to the UFC.

Nearly twenty thousand people erupted. Some booed. Some cheered. Everyone made noise. The boring wrestler had been installed as a nearly three-to-one favorite to pass his first UFC test. Even against a hitman like Robbie Lawler, oddsmakers felt I would be able to dictate what would happen in the fight.

It turned out not to be quite that easy.

I shot in for a double-leg right off the bat against Robbie, and he stopped it. I grabbed his back and draped my weight onto him in a transition when he picked me up on his shoulders and slammed me onto my head. Robbie is really freaking strong, and I have to say, that hurt. I was totally rattled. This was not the start I'd imagined. The fight was fifteen seconds old, and the roof came off the place.

To make matters worse, my wrist was trapped, so Robbie started slamming right hands into my face as I covered up and attempted to regather my wits. I was completely discombobulated, and I think everyone thought the fight was close to being over. He opened up a cut over my left eye and continued to pound away, and all the haters who'd been hoping I'd fall on my face in my UFC debut felt their pulse rise. Joe Rogan, on the pay-per-view broadcast, pointed out that it was the most trouble I'd ever been in in my whole career.[66]

I was in some trouble.

---

66   Joe must not have seen that Lyman Good upkick that knocked me momentarily senseless in Bellator.

But, ever so slowly, through that initial onslaught, I began to recover. I stayed calm and reset enough to begin executing my game plan. From my back, I wrangled Robbie's body with my arms and dragged him in close. I rolled to my side and then onto my knees as Lawler tried to press his elbow through my jugular. Then I got back up, and we clinched over to the fence. The crowd let out a roar. My face was a bloody mess. I'd definitely never been marked up like that in a fight, so it was a scene. The fight was barely sixty seconds in, and it already had a plot twist.

By the two-minute mark Robbie was fending off the takedown.

By the three-minute mark he was on his ass as I went to work.

Within moments, I'd taken his back and begun to sink a rear-naked choke. Robbie squirmed to the side, and now I had him in a bulldog choke, which is a type of headlock. Lawler had his hand up over my head trying to pry loose, and it fell limp and visibly to the ground as I squeezed. I thought, *Shit, he might actually be out!* That's the way it looked to everyone else, too, including referee Herb Dean, who was leaning over the action.

Dean asked Robbie if he was okay, and, when no response came, he jumped in and waved me off, thinking Robbie was unconscious. That's when things went haywire. The instant I released the hold to celebrate, Lawler popped up like a jack-in-the-box to protest. He wasn't out, and there was confusion in the Octagon, not unlike when I beat Ryan Thomas in my Bellator debut some eight years prior.[67] What the hell was going on?

I knew what was going on. I'd won. I'm a defaulting realist, even in the hysteria of a fight. The referee asked Robbie if he was okay and he didn't respond, so Herb's split-second decision to stop the fight was out of my control. That's how it went down, and I was just doing my job.

---

67   Seems I have a knack for debuting controversially.

The crowd, many likely holding bet tickets for the underdog Lawler, didn't particularly care for it. I think I busted some parlays. I told them that they can boo all they want but they're taking their vitriol out on the wrong person, because I'm not the referee. Besides, it wasn't like I wanted it to end like that. Robbie was one of my favorite fighters, and it sucked to have to fight him in my first UFC bout. To end like that was a bummer for me too.

I'd prepared what I was going to say before the fight, which centered around me asking Dana on the hot mic, "Is that the best you got?"...but the situation wasn't quite right for it. When Joe Rogan asked me what I thought happened in the fight after I got my hand raised, I said, "I want to know how long until Dana bitches about that stoppage." Then I said, "I have one other question—Hey, Dana, is that the best you've got? Bring them, baby." The crowd let out a groan. I blew it. I had imagined a cleaner, easier victory to set up the line, and with the fight being as wild as it was, with my face wearing the marks of the battle, the message didn't come off as I'd intended.

I should have pivoted. But I made up for it in the press conference. Robbie had already said his piece to the media and mentioned he'd like a rematch—a sentiment Dana echoed moments later—which was relayed to me by the reporters. Feeling a little bittersweet because my friend Tyron Woodley had lost his welterweight belt just moments before to Marty Usman,[68] I said as bluntly as I could that I'd take a pass on that, because I really hadn't wanted to fight Robbie in the first place. I liked him too much, and the whole situation felt to me like performing a necessary evil. I also criticized Marty's performance against Tyron, mostly to A) plant the seeds for a fight with him in the very near future, and B) because I was so roundly

---

68 I was really mad at the UFC staff, too, who'd promised I could be out there to support him. I skipped getting stitches after my fight to go watch him compete, and they wouldn't allow me back in the arena.

criticized for being boring yet Marty's performance in the biggest fight of his life sucked the air right out of the room. *It was boring as shit.*

I also made it crystal clear what I intended to do next. With my masterplan still very much intact, I'd already booked a trip to London to be cage-side for Darren Till's fight with Jorge Masvidal two weeks later. The London card didn't involve me directly, but then I understood...it was *all* about me. The UFC booked me into a Q&A session while at this event even before my fight with Lawler, because it was all part of the plan. Whoever won the Till-Masvidal fight was going to be a top-five guy, and that's who I wanted to fight next. I viewed them both as fights I should win to catapult to a title shot, and timing-wise, occurring two weeks apart, the schedules meshed nicely.

With the fight being in England, I knew it was set up for Till to showcase, and I really believed that he would win. He had just fought Tyron for a title and didn't have the greatest performance, so I expected him to remedy things in front of his home crowd. The plan was to challenge him on his own turf and make his big moment all about me. In any case, given where both fighters were in the rankings (each in the top five or six), I would be on hand to challenge the winner, right in the heart of Till Country.

I found England to be a great experience, very charming. For the occasion, the UFC made me a Ben "Funky" Askren T-shirt, with the number 84 and Harland on it, in the boutique Roots of Fight style. I stood alongside the soft-spoken Scottish fighter Joanne Calderwood, and Dan Hardy, a retired UK fighter, hosted the session. A solid portion of the fans were drunk at the Q&A and kept yelling, "Hey, you curly-headed fuck!" before asking a question. They were eating out of the palm of my hand.

I riled them up to set the table for a colossal No. 1 contender bout for either June in Chicago or July during International Fight Week in Vegas. Right off the bat, somebody asked me how I felt about a rematch with Lawler, and I said, "I want to fight Darren Till; he's right back there," pointing to where he was. Boos flooded the room, and off we went.

"He's here to cause problems and make some noise; that's what Ben 'Funky' Askren does, we all know that," Hardy said, and on cue Till appeared from behind the curtains flipping me the double birds.

God, it was perfect. Couldn't have gone better.

I made fun of Till's new teeth. Boo! I said if Till's too scared to get in the ring with me, I'd have to come up with a Plan B. Boo! I made fun of a drunk dude in a Hilfiger shirt. Boo! I called the whole gathering dipshits for booing me. Boo! I pointed out that after I beat up Till and did big numbers the UFC would have no choice but to throw me in there with Marty. Boo! I made fun of Ariel Helwani's nose. Cheers.

Soon it was just a bunch of drunken insults, mostly people referring to me as a curly-headed fuck, but I'd done what I'd set out to do—I'd made it so the whole of England now *had* to see Darren Till get his chance to shut me up.

I felt I had to capitalize on the momentum. I wanted to keep things rolling for the fight the next day, so I asked the social media people at the UFC if there was any way they could make a shirt for the event that said "Curly-Headed Fuck" on it. To my immense pleasure, they came through.

I went to the fights the next night, wearing a coat. And when they showed me on the big screen at the O2 Arena there was a raucous chorus of boos. Yet when I opened up my coat to reveal the "Curly-Headed Fuck" shirt, everyone went nuts. The UFC loved it.

This was how to do promotion.

CHAPTER SEVEN:
UNDERSTANDING THE GAME

"Well, that sucked."

—Me, one bad night in July 2019

I fully expected Till to win, but Till didn't win. Till got knocked the fuck out.

Masvidal rushed out like he wanted to do something dramatic to end the fight quickly and ended up slamming a kick into Till's groin. It was a clumsy, unfortunate beginning to the fight, and, in retrospect, slightly portentous. Till looked decent in the first round, but, in the second round, Masvidal clubbed him with a big left hand that dropped him. He followed that up with another left hand while Till lay unconscious on the canvas. So much for baiting England's No. 3–ranked hero into a fight. The crowd in London went silent. Everything just kind of died, including Step Two in my three-step plan to a title shot.

However, all wasn't lost. As I'd had to do my whole career, I just had to modify and revise. Masvidal, who was ranked No. 11 heading into the weekend, cut a nice viral promo just minutes after his fight when he and Leon Edwards got into a backstage scuffle. Leon, a Brit who'd fought Gunnar Nelson in the co-main event that same night at the O2, said something to Masvidal in passing during Jorge's postfight interview backstage. Masvidal heard it, casually walked over to where he stood with his hands behind his back and, without hesitation, unleashed a combination on poor Leon. Masvidal later called it the "three-piece with the soda" when rehashing the episode with ESPN.

Though Masvidal was a respected name, he hadn't quite caught on. He hadn't fought in over a year after tearing his ACL and had recently lost nondescript bouts against Stephen Thompson and Demian Maia. His overall record heading into his fight with Till was 32–13, which wasn't bad by any means, yet, by MMA standards, definitely wasn't all that good.

This was his transformative moment, the moment that people truly *saw* Jorge for the first time, and—more importantly—started to care about him. Not that fans didn't know who he was before, but his biggest claim to fame to that point was that he'd been a bare-knuckle street fighter down in Florida before his career in MMA, just like Kimbo Slice (minus the fanfare). He had a street reputation as mean and nasty, but he wasn't viewed as much of a threat to do anything special in MMA. Now here he was, moments after ruining Till's homecoming party in England with a big knockout, throwing hands at Leon Edwards backstage at the slightest provocation.

I'd say the Cult of Masvidal was born that day.

I registered all this as it unfolded. I knew Jorge was having his moment, and he was getting his first real taste of what it's like to move the needle. He loudly shot into the top five in the welterweight rankings. People were talking about him a lot in the media, zeroing in on his until-then largely ignored Cuban heritage. He was suddenly this Tony Montana figure from Miami, a fighter who was instantly translatable with his zero-fucks-to-give vibe.[69] He was both humanized and mythologized in one unsanctioned backstage encounter with an unsuspecting milquetoast.

All that mattered to me was that Jorge had taken Till's juice.

I knew I had to campaign for a Masvidal fight, but it was a little more complicated than it would've been with Till. I'd already been hounding Till mercilessly in public and all over social media, so I had to restrategize on the fly.[70] The one thing I had in my back pocket was leverage. I was one of the most popular fighters in the UFC, and people were discussing my every move.

With my fight against Robbie having played out in the most wildly absurd and memorable way, I was at the high point of my recognition. Not only had I taken steps to propel that recognition, I stole the show in London, even though I wasn't even competing. I crashed the Till-Masvidal party, like a young Cassius Clay had with Sonny Liston's fight against Floyd Patterson in Las Vegas back in 1963. I did what smart fighters do: I insinuated myself into the conversation.

I kept the fires going on social media, in interviews, anywhere I could. I was playing the game the way it should be played and making myself the attraction.

Yet through this popularity explosion, the truth is I hadn't changed at all. I am who I am, and all my life people either take it or leave it. I was literally the same person I'd always been, only now people wanted to write articles about my tweets. Yet there was a strong feeling of vindication in the air, which amplified my exploits. It was a collective realization that all the lies Dana had perpetuated over the years about me were clearly untrue. He'd said many times, "Askren's dodging the best competition." Yeah, right. I was like Sherman on his march once I made it to the UFC. I was lighting bombs and handing them to every top-five guy in the division, and even

---

69 As instantly as you can translate after a dozen years fighting in major promotions, anyway...

70 Remember, I was in freaking London specifically to egg Till on!

checking the pulse on retired fighters like St-Pierre. My every action further exposed Dana's false narratives, making me a sentimental favorite to anyone who'd been paying attention.

The negative narrative that had been painted about me was disappearing before everybody's eyes, and people recognized that Ben Askren—the real one—was the one chasing his next fight. Jorge had effectively leapfrogged a good portion of the welterweight field, which made him the top, most logical guy for me to go after. And here I was in the catbird seat to egg things on.

The thing was, I really didn't think it could happen.

I assumed Jorge would not want to fight me because of how I dominated in the gym years before in Florida, that he would resist the idea of giving up his newfound shine to get bulldozed by a wrestler. When he beat Till and received the Fight of the Night award from the UFC, I was pretty convinced I wasn't going to get that fight. I began flipping through my mind for a contingency plan. My first thought was maybe Wonderboy Thompson, another top-five guy who was fighting the following week in Nashville against my old Roufusport training partner, Anthony Pettis.

Anthony was moving up to welterweight after a tough stretch at 155 pounds to reinvent himself. Not that I expected him to lose, but logically speaking, going up against Wonderboy...I thought he might be in for a tough night.

Nope. He ended up knocking Thompson out. Good for Anthony!

But so much for fighting Wonderboy.

Now my options were extremely limited. I wasn't going to fight Anthony, of course, and the UFC had already circled Marty Usman's first title defense to be against Colby Covington, so neither was available. I wasn't going to fight my friend Tyron Woodley, either, leaving the same name sitting there in front of me that I'd started with—Jorge Masvidal.

Matchmaking is always a crapshoot in the UFC, and if you're not proactive you end up like Edwards, who relied on words like "deserved" and "meritocracy" to come to his aid when seeking a title bid. It's been proven a million times, but the passive approach just doesn't work.[71] It wasn't my style to leave things to chance. My style was to get what I was after, especially with the clock ticking down on my career.

Strategically, I wanted to get to the title as quickly as I could because I was on borrowed time. My hip was deteriorating by the day. I couldn't run at all in training. All I could do was this pathetic version of a jog that looked more like a hobble, because my hip mobility was so limited. When training jiu-jitsu that spring, my guard was garbage. I couldn't bring my left knee up at all. I was pretty severely hindered from my full range of motion, so I needed to get a fight. Time just wasn't on my side.

As I suspected, Masvidal wasn't into the idea of facing me. He was angling for a Nate Diaz fight, kicking up some dust there to see about an easy payday. Couldn't blame him, to be honest. I'd have lobbied for Diaz over Ben Askren, too. But there was something else at the heart of his hesitation that I knew full well was going on.

Other fighters were put off by the amount of publicity I was getting with just one UFC fight. They genuinely resented it, because they'd been in the UFC a lot longer, and here I was making more money and generating more media than them. Masvidal, who had busted out of a decades-long anonymity shell in one weekend, was no different. When asked about fighting me next, he shrugged it off. He said something along the lines of, "Fuck that dude," implying that he had no interest in fighting an undeserving (as he called me) "social media guy." The attitude in the air was that I hadn't done enough to even warrant having my name mentioned with theirs, which sounded to me like more residual noise from Dana's echo chamber.

---

71   Leon even botched a silver-platter fight with Masvidal after their little backstage melee by not playing his cards right. The man couldn't get out of his own way. The moral of the story: never be like Leon.

So, I did what I'd been doing since college. I provoked the shit out of him.

Just as I'd done with Till, I put out Instagram posts stirring things up. I let everyone know how easily I'd handled Jorge in the gym down in Florida a decade before when I was a novice starting out and made it clear it wouldn't be all that hard to do it again. I said that of course he wouldn't want to fight me, because he knew damn well how it would go. If he signed on the dotted line, he would meet a predictable fate. Nobody likes to take an inevitable beating.

On and on. With that constant baiting, the public demand for the fight ratcheted up. I'd been poking the bear, and now the bear was starting to growl. Some people wanted Jorge to shut me up. With MMA fans forever obsessed with who is going to fight whom next, it was great theater, and things were escalating.

A couple of weeks later, I think Masvidal finally saw the light.

He understood how big of a fight he had on his hands against a polarizing figure like me, who commanded the fight public's attention. He accepted the fight, which was set to take place at UFC 239 on July 6 in Vegas, the big summer event to cap off International Fight Week.

Just as it had been when I fought Robbie, my second UFC fight would be the swing bout on a pay-per-view with a pair of title fights. This time Jon Jones was defending his title against Thiago Santos, and women's bantamweight champion Amanda Nunes was fighting Holly Holm. In a weird way, I was being asked to sell Jon Jones's pay-per-view yet again, which was fine by me.

Jorge was a guy I knew I could beat. Better yet, Jorge was like a ticking time bomb, at least to the public's way of seeing things. With Robbie, the perception was that I was messing with a cold-blooded killer whose blank expressions could be translated as impending doom, but with Jorge I was dealing with a hot-blooded Cuban who felt generally disrespected.

He'd gone years in the game as a capable B-side, but realistically he was the penultimate fighter. He never came in first. He always came up a little short. He had weaknesses in his game that fighters had exploited time and again, weaknesses that played directly to my strengths.

Given the heightened stakes and Masvidal's now fully realized South Beach gangster chic, this was as much a clash of personality types as it was contenders. He was a smirking guy in Versace who would make throat-slashing gestures with his tongue out. I was a Midwestern guy in flip-flops with a Wisconsin accent who just loved getting under his skin. The general interest among fight fans was piqued by these aesthetics alone. Jorge's freshly grown-out hair had people rechristening him "Street Jesus," which he ran to the bank with.

I just made fun of him. It was too easy.

I embraced being the guy that people loved to hate, especially among the fighters. It bothered Jorge the whole way. He kept trying to say I was Dana's favorite in the buildup to the fight, and I was like, "What the fuck are you *talking* about— have you not paid attention to anything? I am the *farthest* thing from being the teacher's pet in the UFC!" My feud with Dana wasn't only well documented, it was still active. How neglected must Jorge have felt to play that tone-deaf angle in the media?

I knew one thing, though: Jorge was a good foil to me. And I was a good foil to him.

In fighting, every great champion needs a foil at the critical moment that people are paying attention. Back when Anderson Silva was defending the middleweight title against every woodwork contender the UFC could dredge up, he was a big-ticket curiosity in the UFC. But he became a *star* when irreverent Chael Sonnen came along and gave everyone a strong emotional investment in the fight. While everyone else had been somewhere between reverent and "in awe" of Silva, Chael did everything in his power to discount the greatest fighter of that era. People ate it up. He paid Silva no respect whatsoever. He was a promo machine, a pro wrestler who could actually wrestle, which was a weakness of Silva's. Whether people loved this tactic or hated it, they cared enough to pay the premium to see how it would play out at UFC 117 (and again for the rematch at UFC 148). Chael changed the game by being a foil to Silva, and by doing so he put Anderson Silva into a different strata of stardom.[72]

It's not rocket science. Years later I did a podcast with my friend Front Row Brian citing the top ten personalities in MMA. What the podcast ended up being about was how certain people help other people shine. I don't think there was anyone on that top personality list who was on an island by him- or herself. Every great personality in the sport had a counterpart, somebody to play off against, somebody who cast doubt over their greatness, somebody who forced them to rise to the occasion, and the interactions between them helped grow both followings.

The obvious example is Ali and Frazier, looking back at how much they needed each other in the 1970s to become who they became. People saw conflicts in a boxing match that superseded two guys throwing punches at each other. Foils in fighting are imperative, to the point that the fight itself takes on broader cultural conflict. Like with Joe Louis and Max Schmeling. More was at stake, and both guys knew it. Nate Diaz and Conor McGregor, another good one. Jon Jones and Daniel Cormier brought the best and worst out of each other. Their rivalry got so heated and personal that it unfolded like a saga in the daily tabloids. Things blew up big when that behind-the-scenes banter between them before a televised interview was accidentally leaked, showing their true feelings. That interaction gave depth to the rivalry and introduced the genuine element of hatred.

But it has to be organic.

---

72 Remember when Anderson was supposedly learning techniques from Steven Seagal? Or when he faced Demian Maia at UFC 112 and it came closer to performance art than it did a fight? He was headed straight toward gimmickry before Chael came along. Dana was even turning on him!

You can't foster genuine bad blood. You can't call some-body out and try to tether yourself to their elevated station unless you have something to round out that equation...a backstory with them, an ongoing feud, a general distaste of who they are as a human being. That's why my feud with Dana was such a strong subplot throughout my career. I genuinely didn't care for how he did business, and that had been known for years.

Masvidal benefitted a ton by having me stoke the fires for our fight at UFC 239. Even with just one UFC fight under my belt I had way more juice than him (which made him mad), and we had a now very public backstory (which made him madder). I benefitted as well, because Masvidal's fuck-all atti-tude became the costar in the festivities. He genuinely wanted to kick my ass, and he let the public share in that desire. I was in heaven.

We were mutually beneficial to each other.

And it made for a big fight. How big?

Big enough that for the first time ever the UFC included the third bout in the promos. Generally the UFC promo videos for pay-per-views highlight the main event with a secondary spotlight cast onto the co-main event, espe-cially when there are two title fights. But for this one, Jorge and I had a whole chunk of the UFC 239 promo dedicated to our fight. They knew the hook in play for the card, the added dimension that would make people splurge for the purchase. Our fight was overshadowing two consensus GOATs in Jones and Nunes. And there was legitimate tension in the air. Each time Jorge and I were in the same room during fight week people worried about a confronta-tion. Would Jorge fly off the handle and sock me? Would I provoke him to the point where he lost his shit? My casual nature only seemed to irk him more, and people were glued to us like we were a two-man soap opera.

The only thing left to do was to go out and fight.

The game plan was the same as always—take him down and dominate him for as long as I needed to. If it ain't broke, don't fix it. Jorge was the fight I wanted because his takedown defense wasn't that great. I knew I could control him there, as I had many other fighters. It was my tried-and-true formula for winning, and I was prepared to do it again.

People have asked me what I remember about the fight?
Nothing.
I remember entering the cage and eyeing him up, and then Bruce Buffer's introductions. I remember the ref saying "fight," and then my next connected memory was when I woke up, I was in the hospital. I don't remember the ambulance ride *to* the hospital or even walking out of the cage (which somehow I did). I don't remember anything. When I snapped back into full consciousness, there were white walls and bright lights. I didn't know where the hell I was. I remember seeing Luke Rockhold, who'd been brutally knocked out by Jan Błachowicz earlier on the card. That's when it dawned on me that I must be in the hospital.
Then I saw my brother Max, along with Amy.
She said something like, "Do you remember what happened?" I said, "Well, I'm in the hospital, and I'm not sore or sweaty...so whatever happened happened fast, and it couldn't have been good if I am here."
They filled me in on what happened.
Jorge perfectly timed a flying knee just as I was shooting in for a takedown, it landed, and—*boom*—I was out. The entire fight took only five seconds, the quickest in UFC history. He landed a couple of follow-up shots while I was unconscious on the canvas. It was a lot to hear and try to stitch back together. When most people have a bad day at the office, they have a recollection as to what happened to make it that

way. They may *intentionally* try to block it out, but it's in there somewhere. I didn't have that.

When I was told all of this none of it rang a bell. It sucked. For a guy who can instantly recall granular details of a fight or wrestling match or a game of disc golf from a decade earlier by flipping to a file in my brain, all I had to work with was a pothole in time on this one. As I got checked out, I had to catch up to the disappointment. My first loss as a cagefighter was as if it happened to someone else. It was like fiction that had to be real.

But in a situation like that, a lot of thoughts flood your head afterward. Boring fighter? Ha! I was now involved in two of the craziest fights of 2019, both in the UFC. This one was at my expense, but boring my ass. Sadder thoughts creep in, too, the reality of the situation as obvious as the light shining in my eye. My route to a UFC title was blown to bits. I'd need to revise. My last legit shot at winning a UFC title was gone. My hips would not allow me to start over to get there again; I knew that much.

And of course, I knew people were talking.

People talked about the knockout for the next week.

People talked about that knockout for the rest of the year.[73] My haters had a day. To some, it was a comeuppance. It was part of the psychological makeup of the fight; you talk a big game, the onus always falls to you to back it up. I knew that, of course. I talked a big game, so everyone had the right to give it back. But some of my haters' victory laps lasted for years, because when you have no life of your own you magnify the failures of those who do.

The replay of it was everywhere. As I write this, there are no less than seven billion gifs of it, so I can't help but relive it all day, all night, over the holidays, at my daughter's birthday party, wherever it comes across my phone. I could tweet out that "grass is green" and somebody will inevitably respond with that gif of Jorge's knee crashing into my head.

---

73   Hell, people still talk about the knockout just as much today as they did in 2019.

It's tweeted ad nauseam.

The UFC uses it on an endless loop in its promo videos for Masvidal.

It's everywhere.

And I live with it. For a guy who couldn't remember what happened, nobody is likely to ever let me forget that it did. Because I was one of the most boisterous personalities on social media in the UFC, that night people were anxious to see how I'd respond. The only time I opened up my phone at all that night was to tweet out the three words that captured my version of events perfectly.

"Well, that sucked."

That lightened the mood.

It did suck.

The one thing that annoyed me after watching the actual fight played back was the fact that Jorge punched me—*twice*—when I was already out on the canvas. All I could think was, *What kind of degenerate does that?* Yet the fact that he did only served to make the Cult of Masvidal that much bigger. When he was asked if the extra shots were necessary in the postfight press conference, Jorge responded with his now-famous quip, "It was super necessary."

That response has since blown up into a hashtag.

And even though I thought it was cowardly to throw those punches on a defenseless fighter, I had to admit that response was kind of funny. I'd egged Jorge on pretty well in the lead-up to the fight, so he felt justified in getting the last laugh. He had the media eating out of the palm of his hand. He had taken my juice, and he knew it.

Meanwhile, I was left to think about stuff that couldn't be repaired. Things that happened. Things that were said and/or ignored.

A couple of weeks earlier during a training session, I remembered saying to my training partner Mike "Biggie" Rhodes, "I know he's going to try something crazy right away," recalling what he did to Darren Till when he kicked him in the nuts in the opening seconds. It was a big moment, and Jorge would try to make a splash. Rhodes mentioned that it might be a flying knee, which I pondered momentarily before letting it go in one ear and out the other. Flying knees so rarely work I didn't give it much thought. Besides, if he did that he would leave himself vulnerable. I could dodge it and have an easier entry point for a takedown. But the prevailing feeling was he might try something crazy right out of the gate, and—as I'd done as a competitor my whole life—I left it to my own intuition to get out of the way of whatever that was going to be.

As I've mentioned earlier, I'm not a fan of excuses, and I don't bother with regrets. What's the point? But I do wish I could remember exactly that split second before the knee landed and identify whatever reason my body didn't adjust to the incoming stimulus. I am obsessed with details. Sequences. Puzzles. As a wrestler on the spectrum, I could visualize certain moments in time and what it felt like, and why I made certain decisions. It's like slow motion replay in my own mind. Even with my next opponent, Demian Maia, I can easily ratio-nalize everything I did and remember my thinking precisely at any given moment of that fight, as if dialing back into the exact frequency of the sequential thought.

But for Masvidal, I don't have that memory, so I can't make that judgment on why. Rationally and logically, I can try. I know my mobility was so compromised that if you rewatch the takedown with Jorge (and with Robbie, for that matter), my penetration steps for wrestling were limited. There wasn't any explosion. I hinged almost exclusively with my back over right, rather than squatting with my knees bent. In a text-book takedown, you bend your knees so that your chest comes closer, and your hips close a little more. I couldn't do that, and it didn't help.

Really, though, it was the foreign nature of the move.

Usually with a flying knee it's punch, punch, then jump knee, not covering as much distance. But a running flying knee didn't really happen. I misjudged everything because of the speed with which he was coming at me. My body and mind didn't react because it was for me an original sequence. I had never reacted to it before, had no muscle memory, and therefore it didn't compute.

I can say this, though: your body develops patterns from training and, as far as instincts go, most instincts are developed in practice. Instincts aren't developed in competition; instincts are developed through countless repetitions in practice. No one throws a running flying knee like that with any serious hope of it working.

But Jorge did.

And it worked. It was a perfect storm. Had it not worked, he would've been on his back fending off elbows and hammerfists. Gratifying as it might've felt to some, it had nothing to do with emotion. It had nothing to do with him being mad at me for provoking him so mercilessly in the lead-up. To this day it cracks me up when people say things like that.

Come on.

I *wanted* to get him mad, because, in most cases, a mad fighter doesn't perform at his optimal best. Decades of wrestling at a high level taught me that. You want to be even keel in combat competition, and if you can rattle your opponent, great. Manipulating emotion is all part of the gamesmanship in MMA, but to not be affected is a lesson in sports psychology. Obviously it didn't work out well for me in this case, but I never understood people who say things like, "Oh, well, you never should have talked shit!"

Really? You're telling me that a professional fighter who's paid to do their job, which is to go beat somebody up, is going to do his job *better* just because I said some words? Shouldn't they just be performing their best no matter what? Do they really have to have extra motivation to do their jobs at the highest level possible, or should they show up and compete no matter what? People who say such things are idiots.

There's no such thing as poking the bear if you're not overly concerned with the bear coming after you in anger. No, I just fucked the fight up is all. It so happened to be a big fight with good hysteria surrounding it. A fight that everyone was watching with rooting interests, financial stakes, emotional investments, and a large dose of poetic justice. It was big enough to ruin my plans and reconfigure the welterweight division. Big enough to make Jorge into a celebrity, and to start up his own mescal company. It was big enough for then-President Donald Trump to treat Jorge as a hero and get him involved with his 2020 campaign.[74] It was a big enough fight for Jorge to get a headlining spot at Madison Square Garden a few months later, and for the UFC to invent a belt for his headlining fight with Nate Diaz to provide a sense of magnitude.

The "Baddest Motherfucker" (BMF) title became a thing because of my fight with Jorge. Madison Square Garden was Step Three in my three-step plan. I had envisioned fighting for the UFC title there when I came over in the trade. But all that was gone in five seconds. Part of the beauty of fighting has always been its cruelty.

So much floods your mind when you go back over a knockout again and again with so much missing data. Then the doctor comes in and says that your scans came back fine, there's no damage, and you're free to go. And you're in Las Vegas, and the town is still jumping, and you realize you still have an afterparty to attend. At the goddamn Paris Hotel.

I was being paid to attend it, so I had to go. We left the hospital and reentered the traffic of life, where everybody was out partying on a Saturday night, their fortunes and fates still very much on track. The music was loud, and the lights were bright. Talk about a depressing afterparty. A lot of my friends

---

74 Donald referred to the fight a lot on the trail, but my favorite was when he retold the story that Jorge was fighting this "young superstar who was going to be great...who was supposed to be the future of the UFC." For a long time thereafter I changed my Twitter name to "Young Superstar," because you've got to have a sense of humor in this game.

were there, and the urges to comfort me were well intended. Everyone wanted to come up and give their condolences, to tell me it was okay, but I didn't really need it. Just like when I came up short at the Olympics, I understood life can move only in one direction. Losing happens, but dwelling on it is what defines a loser.

I didn't want people feeling bad for me. I knew the score.

To compete at the highest levels of combat sports is a balance, and losing sits heavy on the one side of the ledger. For your first loss to become a viral meme is hard. I'm not going to lie—it sucks. But, to play the game right, you have to have a thick skin. That so many people wanted to rub it in my face only served as proof that they were invested. They cared.

If I had won—and I really believe that if Jorge and I fought a hundred times, I'd have won ninety-nine of those—I'd have fought for a title in the fall of 2019. But if I was going to lose, I wanted to lose well. I would not make excuses, and in my heart of hearts I had no regrets. Plus, the rational side of my brain never stops working.

How bad could it be? I had already retired once, contentedly, so wasn't all of this a kind of bonus episode to my competitive life?

Did I lose what I had been chasing for a long time? I did.

But the thing is, I just made $200,000 to fight for five seconds. Is it really that bad? Is my life really that bad? Do I still have my family? Do I have my wrestling academies? My health? I was fine.

I really was. What's weird is, after watching the tape of the fight, I think Jorge may have hit me on the neck rather than the face. I never had a headache. I went to the afterparty, where the lights were bright and the music was blaring, but they didn't affect me at all. When I went to bed that night, no headache. I didn't have one when I woke up, either. I was fine.

Still, the whole thing sucked.

CHAPTER EIGHT:
ATTITUDE

*"Every fighter's only as good as their last performance.
You have a great performance, everyone thinks
you're the champ. You look like shit,
everyone tells you you suck."*

—Me

Everyone loses.

It happens to everyone in every walk of life, to every great human who ever breathed the air on this Earth. It happens in competition, especially, where by design one side wins and the other side gets a dose of reality.[75] Losing in fighting is part of the game, and I knew that, even if I truly believed I could retire undefeated. But I played the game well, and I let people feast on my undefeated record, for as long as it lasted, in whatever way they wanted. In prizefighting, the longer you can remain unbeaten the longer people kick around delusional terms like "invincible," because no other sport budgets for such extreme levels of hyperbole.

But *nobody* is invincible, not Israel Adesanya, not Floyd Mayweather, not Muhammad Ali or Bruce Lee or Cael Sanderson. In fact, that word is nothing more than a temptation to

---

75 Except in soccer, where ties are tolerated. And in Metamoris, a jiu-jitsu promotion where pretty much every match ended in a stalemate.

any competitor who hears it. It's a thing to be debunked for all the world to see, to prove whoever is using such a stupid word a fool.

It's why in my ultimate plan of plans I would've run through the guys I needed to in the UFC's welterweight ranks, won the belt, and then tried to lure long-time champion Georges St-Pierre out of retirement for my swan-song fight. I would've loved to show that Georges was all-too-vincible on my way out. And for that matter, Khabib too.

As Ric Flair famously said, "To be the man, you gotta beat the man."

That's just the nature of being a competitor.

I'd lost a fight, but a high-profile loss in MMA, even after getting devoured by public opinion, can still be a net gain. In Vegas, the house loses plenty, but the house is always a winner. The big picture in prizefighting is no different. I lost to Masvidal in a very public, fairly humiliating way, yet I did what I had to—I went onto Ariel Helwani's show on ESPN the Monday after to talk about it. Only thirty-six hours had passed, but showing up to address it was important to me. I didn't need to cower behind a wounded ego, because it's MMA. As everybody knows, shit happens in MMA! In some ways, mixed martial arts is nothing more than chaos with a referee. All through my competitive life, I had made a point of maintaining separation between ego and outcome. Losing wasn't the end of the world. I was the same guy. I knew people would want to hear from me, but really I'm incapable of being anything other than I am. Besides, I understood better than anyone that there were shitty ways to lose.

A classic example was Ronda Rousey.

Ronda didn't admit anything after getting knocked out by Holly Holm at UFC 193, nor did she speak to the media in the aftermath. She handled it pretty horribly for an athlete of her standing, and, by that time, she'd become a fixture of pop culture. Beyoncé was out there quoting her at concerts, and girls everywhere were getting into judo and MMA because of her. She was like the Royce Gracie of women's MMA. She was everywhere.

Yet, in getting thoroughly destroyed by Holly in front of fifty-six thousand people down in Australia (plus millions more around the world), she became the exact opposite of who she portrayed herself to be while she was winning. She'd lived cozily within the public's perception of her own invincibility—she'd been called the Mike Tyson of WMMA—and tricked herself into believing it. Consequently, she showed no resolve to bounce back stronger after being humbled. She didn't admit to herself that she wasn't as good as she'd thought she was. She didn't try to learn from it.

The truth is, the UFC had built up Ronda to impossible, unsustainable levels, which, for anyone who understands the game, is an enviable position. People were saying she could "beat Floyd Mayweather" in a fight and claiming she could be a "world champion boxer." For a judoka who hadn't been tested all that much, it was a wild collective flight of fancy, but Ronda basked in the attention. After being humbled, she should've undergone a personal reevaluation, admitting that, "Hey, maybe I bought into my own hype, and now I need to go back to the drawing board..."

But she couldn't do that. She was just done.[76]

My situation wasn't *exactly* like that, other than our losses were momentous occasions in the fight world that endured in the public's imagination, eventually cornering the market in memes.

---

76 Literally—she competed just one more time, and it wasn't much of a fight. It came thirteen months later against Amanda Nunes, a bout in which Ronda was allowed to forego all media requests beforehand—an unprecedented stipulation for a UFC main-event fighter. After she got blown up in that fight she simply quit. She went on to married life and pro wrestling. She was still under thirty years old at the time. I'd never argue against anybody getting out of the fight game while still young and vital, because there are truly so few graceful outs, but to reach such a peak in a nascent sport and then have such a precipitous drop-off...it was unparalleled. In fact, it was damn near unimaginable.

I said I was better than Jorge, and I believe(d) I really was both in heart and mind. You play that scenario out again—or look at it as a series, through the lens of averages—I win that fight the vast majority of the time. My greatest strengths played directly to his most glaring weaknesses.[77] Anyone with any small amount of fight acumen could've seen that. That's why I was a prohibitive favorite.

But again, frustrating as it was, is, and continues to be, MMA is insane and shit happens.

The question was: How was I going to deal with it?

I'd always taken everything I could from a loss to make it mean something. I dealt with setbacks throughout high school, while wrestling early on at Mizzou, and finally at the Beijing Olympics. All of them sucked. You think you're really good until somebody proves otherwise, leaving you only one real course of action: get back to work and get better, fix what went wrong.

My failures at each stop became my strengths as I went through my competitive life. They were necessary because I made damn sure to see them that way. It's a cliché in fighting that too many don't actually believe, but the idea is to learn from every failure. If you can rid your mind of self-delusion, that's even better. You see it with local MMA fighters who think they're way better than they really are as they come up. If what you're saying before a fight is way off from the actual reality, there needs to be a recognition of that fact—a kind of reset.

I didn't *want* to talk about the Masvidal loss thirty-six hours after it happened, but I did because I wanted to show I am the exact same guy win or lose. It was uncomfortable to an extent. After a decade of winning, I was used to talking about what went right before planting the seeds for my next fight. This time I just told it like it was. I said I had nothing to hide from. Mistakes happen. I'd joined the ranks of the defeated in

---

77   I know, I know, small consolations for the ever-reasoning mind. But a five-second KO is the definition of getting caught.

pro MMA, which, if anything, gave me fraternity. These were real feelings. I think the fight public appreciated that I was exactly the same matter-of-fact guy.

Realistically, I was. A lot of people talk about the weight of the "zero," meaning how heavy the "0" on your undefeated record becomes. Not for me. I carried it lightly the whole way. If I felt invulnerable, it was because I trained so hard and left as little as I could to chance. But I never felt unbeatable. I trained harder than anybody else *because* I knew that. I think that's what pissed some people off and ultimately gave them joy when I fell. I *was* beatable, but for nearly a decade in MMA nobody could actually beat me.

I said it wasn't a relief to finally lose. Hell no! I would've happily carried the "zero" off into retirement in Hartland and figuratively hung it on my wall for decoration.

I answered all Ariel's questions with the same no-bullshit approach as I'd have taken if I'd won. Facts are facts. For nine years I had said I wanted to prove that I was the best, and when I got to the doorstep of proving it I came up short. Those were the facts, and facts are indifferent to our emotions.

After that interview, as the gifs of the KO flooded my social media feed, I got back to life. I had been building a disc golf course on my property at home, in which one of the hazards became my old Prius car from college, a backboard on hole 20 called "the island hole," and I had five-time world champ Paul McBeth come over and play it.[78] My kids at the academy were doing well, and it was an easy place to divert my competitive juices. We had a strong tournament in Fargo with our kids in the program. I kept stoking the fires on social media, too.

I tweeted out an apology to the public at large for having lost, because now everyone would be subjected to the mind-numbingly bland back-and-forth between Marty Usman and Colby Covington before their fight. What a snoozefest I'd left the fight world to deal with.

---

78 Later, in May 2020, he came back with Brodie Smith, when the disc tour was cancelled due to COVID.

"I want to apologize for losing because now all of you have to listen to Marty and Colby talk trash to each other," I tweeted. "It will be damn near unbearable." I said that to lighten the mood. In an interview later on, I compared them to two sixth graders on the playground, with one saying, "Hey, you wanna go?" and the other saying, "Hell yeah, do it, let's go," and the other replying, "Okay, cool, do something." On and on. I guaranteed we'd all lose multiple IQ points listening to those idiots argue, and I should have done my part to help avoid it.

I was having fun. I wasn't sulking. People appreciated it.

I was also plotting my next course of action, training as much as my body would allow as frequently as I could.

Though the setback dropped me momentarily out of shouting distance of a title shot, I knew that two wins in a row could get me back in the picture quick. MMA wasn't built like boxing, where if you lose you're cast into fight purgatory, buried by the stigma of the failure. In MMA, you're never too far away as long as you're in demand, especially when the UFC's fight schedule marches on so mercilessly, which can't help but favor the prepared. I was still popular, and I was always prepared. I just needed to win a couple in a row and to keep my name in the conversation.

When I began talking to the matchmakers at the UFC, I tossed Darren Till's name out there one more time as a possible opponent—go for the easy money, you know?—but when they countered with the soft-spoken Demian Maia, I was okay with it.

I had half-heartedly called Demian out when I got to the UFC, which wasn't anything personal—I'd called out all the top guys. If anything, I liked Demian and had a ton of respect for him. He'd fought for a belt three times in his career. He was quietly good and at times genuinely *great*, a kind of silent assassin. But the reason I really liked him was that he was one of the few jiu-jitsu guys who effectively and dedicatedly added wrestling to his game while sticking to his roots. In fact, he might be the *only* one to do that. He'd managed to keep an oath to those roots by never straying from what he was, which was a really high-level grappler.

I could relate, because I'd done the same by adding submission grappling to the thing I did best: wrestling. He was an ambassador of jiu-jitsu, and I kept the singlet close. In the world of MMA, we flew these flags as our whole identity.

Demian was ranked a spot or two above me, so the fight made sense to my revised plan. It would take place on October 26, as a five-round main event in Singapore. The UFC needed a big attraction for that foreign Fight Night, so why not have me return to my ONE Championship playground? I was more than happy to go back to one of the places I love most in the world. I was undefeated there in my previous three visits. So I had nothing but good experiences there.

It was a fascinating matchup, too—a world-class submission grappler against a pure wrestler who wouldn't be afraid to play in those deep waters. If I took Demian down, wouldn't I be inviting myself into a hazard area? Wouldn't I be begging him to torque a limb off my body or snatch my neck? There would be precise ground skills on display, perhaps so high level as to outpace the judges' ability to comprehend what it was they'd be seeing. It was an MMA hipster's delight. It would be takedowns versus submission attempts versus reversals versus ground-and-pound—an ouroboros of a fight, with no small amount of judging subjectivity. As for potential scrambles? MMA purists were writing entire think pieces about how those might play out.

If you'd watched Demian's fights over the years, you knew he couldn't get swayed into a stand-and-bang brawl under some pretense that he should, though he was cerebral enough to effectively incorporate all styles around his base. That included purposeful boxing, similar to me.

I loved the matchup. I think the majority of the fight public liked the idea, too. After I'd been knocked out by Masvidal in what everyone saw as the most vicious way possible, Demian was being perceived as a soft landing spot. One writer had called him "the closest thing to a pacifist as you'll find in MMA," given his penchant for submitting people in lieu of butchering them. Demian wasn't out to hurt people.

I was thirty-five years old and still had five fights left on my contract, while Demian was six years *older* than me and making one last good push. To the fight public, it was two twilight competitors in an extremely relevant fight for the title picture. Demian had won two in a row, having just come off a victory over Anthony Rocco Martin. I was coming off my first-ever loss, and I got caught. Both of us were right there in the welterweight title picture.

Though I obviously didn't make a big deal of it, the only problem was that my hips were getting progressively worse. When I rowed, I couldn't bring my knees all the way to my chest, I couldn't run, and I was limited in what I could do on the mats. I couldn't do a regular sit-up because my labrum was torn. It progressed negatively faster than I wanted, and I had an MRI done in mid-September of that year to get some clarity. Before getting back the results, my doctor, Bus Tarbox in Columbia, said best-case scenario was there might be a minor surgical procedure that could be done to help extend my career a bit, which gave me some optimism.

However, when I noticed he was kind of avoiding me over the next couple of weeks whenever I pressed him for the results, I took it as an ominous sign.[79] I knew I'd fight Demian no matter what, so it ultimately didn't matter what the results were in the short term. Even if I had to fight on crutches, I was headed to Singapore to keep my appointment.

In spite of all this, my training camp was actually very good. I brought in a world-class BJJ champion, Dan Borovic, and we

---

79   I suspected that what he discovered was that there wasn't going to be any minor fix and he was letting me have my last hurrah. In any case, I did what I did back in high school when the doctor warned if I competed I would risk paralysis: I put it out of my head and trained for my fight.

trained a shit-ton of jiu-jitsu. I had taken to jiu-jitsu so thoroughly that I relished the opportunity to try myself against a master like Maia.

I wasn't kidding myself. I knew that if things didn't go my way, this could very well be my last fight. So, my new battle plan was similar to the original plan I put together when I came over to the UFC, with a couple of key modifications and extensions.

I knew there was a fight card set to take place just six weeks later in Washington, DC, which was in need of a headliner. I circled it and mentally slotted myself into that main event, figuring I'd lobby for it in the postfight interview after I beat Demian. Demian wasn't a marauder in the way Lawler was, and he wasn't as tempestuous as Masvidal. He was more of a martial artist. I calculated I could get through the fight relatively unscathed, if I dictated the action as I'd done so many times in the past. I wasn't looking past Demian so much as preparing myself mentally and physically for a quick return. I wanted to fight for a title in the first half of 2020. There was no time to waste.

The lead-up to fight night was far quieter than it had been back in July when Jorge and I fought in Vegas. For that one, the tension had revved to the red, and our every move had been documented by the media. For Demian, who is super-reserved and respectful, it was a breeze, especially with the fight on the other side of the planet where the media contingency wasn't all that much. The lack of tension was kind of a relief, to be honest. One thing I'd learned during my time with ONE Championship was that you don't need to hate your opponents. Though it's a fun dimension for fans and the actual promotion of a fight, it's really not necessary. I didn't actually hate anybody in the UFC,[80] though I think there were some fighters who hated me. Not in this case. The mutual respect between Demian and me became the subplot of the fight.

---

80   Though I think if I could've fought Dillon Danis—a little runt in Bellator who'd built his name off Conor McGregor—around this time, I'd have ragdolled him with a little extra relish. I hated him in the way people hate flies in their living room.

Yet, as happens with fights with a highly anticipated dimension—for this one, *what happens when the fight hits the canvas?*—in the opening round we spent most of the time on our feet. I did what I'd always done best, which was pressure Demian from the word go. When there was a potential lag, I pressured him some more. Disruption was the key. It had always worked. It had been the hallmark of my wrestling style. I'd be so relentless that I'd make you make a mistake or simply put you in a situation you didn't want to be in. It was one of the first things I got really good at, and even in a fight where my hips were degenerative and I couldn't do all I wanted, I believed I could still outwork anybody.

Demian connected with a straight left. I landed a solid uppercut and soon got him in the clinch. He got out, but I was constantly closing the distance. My constant was to be constant. One of the things I eventually created, in addition to ensuring superior cardio as I got better at scrambling in college, was the concept of mental taxation. If you watch fighting enough, you see clearly that people fight in spurts. They come forward throwing, then have a natural instinct to take a break. This happens in wrestling, too.

I realized at some point that these breaks are both physical *and* mental. They are a quick mental reset to say, okay, I'm going to tie up this way, then do this or that. A break is the mind's natural moment to regather. I realized if I wrestled without mental breaks in practice, I was teaching myself how to become relentless through those spaces. A cruel, nonstop machine that overwhelms the need to regroup. If I practiced it enough, it would become normal for me to push through mental and physical breaks and do what nobody else does.

That is, just keep coming.

Disrupting.

Breaking the guy in front of me.

Demian landed a right hand that connected solid. I dirty boxed in close, hitting him with some short uppercuts. I marked him up pretty good in the first round and took him down with about forty-five seconds left. The crowd let up a roar when he tried a straight armlock, but I knew it wasn't there.

The secret to the funky style was prohibiting my opponents from regaining their own conventions and agency. I practiced this endlessly. I spent years torturing myself in training so that I could create havoc for whoever faced me. Confuse the muscle memory. Scramble their bearings. Why did I seem so casual and carefree in a tense atmosphere of high-level athletes? Because I knew what I'd put myself through to become who I was. You take that mental break away, that little reset that the mind needs, the guy is mentally fucked. *He is mentally fucked.*

God, I loved the moments when that became clear.

I knew it throughout my competitive life. That moment the guy begins to drown from the pressure. I'd taught myself early to be the tide. I was the tide.

The second round, I won on all scorecards.

I began to get into a rhythm.

I've always been a slow starter, but once I get rolling I know how to use the momentum. Demian's face was bloodied. I was flinging punches and catching him on retreats. I shot in with a little over a minute remaining, and we went into a scramble. He tried a triangle before transitioning into an omoplata, which I reversed. Now the fight was playing out as advertised, as a frenetic chess match on the ground. We scrambled again, and I reversed. The round ended. John Gooden, the commentator for the fight, said we had a first course of striking and now a main course of grappling.

Whatever the analogy, I'd been in the quicksand with Maia, and I'd survived, just like I knew I would.

Now it was time to drag him into my own deep waters.

I tripped and threw him down hard a minute into the third round. He was able to get up. Demian was tough. He had tricks, and he had heart. I took him down on a single-leg, and he reversed. He went to full mount, then took my back as I rolled to my side to scramble out. I grabbed his wrist and torqued it away above my head, but he's slick...

Over the course of the fight, any fight, I'd simply overwhelm. Hit me, kick me, bite me, pull my hair, I would still become the tide. I was going to wear Demian down. That's the dogged nature of a wrestler; more directly, that's the stubborn application of the will that I brought to a fight. You cannot outwork me. You train for every situation. You train away nerves. Repetition steels you for everything you could possibly encounter. Countless hours on the mats when everyone else is out having fun. Life wasn't out there. Life was on those mats.

He got a body triangle.

He slammed a couple of punches into the side of my head from his position in the back. Then he just as fluidly sank a rear-naked choke, and the natural order of things began to dissipate...it was deep...I caught a glimpse of the lights above, blurring to watery darkness, and after all those thousands of hours killing myself to keep it in my favor, control very peacefully left my grips.

I tapped just once before I went out.

The bus ride back to the hotel after losing wasn't a particularly long one, but it felt like it dragged on for a million miles. All these stupid scenarios and reflections. In my calculating mind, I was doing the daunting math. With back-to-back losses, I'd need to win three or four fights in a row to get a title shot. There's no way my hips would allow that. The elusive goal of winning a UFC title had now slipped around the bend and was no longer in sight, which left me with an empty feeling. Already in a low mood, I called Dr. Tarbox and I said, "I know you've been avoiding me, so now that my fight's done give me the prognosis on my hips."

He confirmed what I suspected to be the case, and—realistically—what I felt every time I tried to run or bend. There would be no quick fix to extend my shelf life as a fighter. I would need full-on hip replacement surgery, the sooner the better. He said if I felt like I was tough enough to endure the chronic pain, I could keep fighting, but the reality was that nothing could be done until I got a Birmingham hip, which is a metal-on-metal joint that allows for normal motion.

That was it. I knew it was over.

I had come to the UFC with one goal in mind: to win the title. With no short-term fix available, and with the title now so far away, I knew I was at the end of the road.

It's hard to accept things like that. There were definitely some "what ifs."

Those what ifs are trouble. They are persistent. Private. Convincing. They are poetic in how they present themselves, trying to justify the things that went wrong, seeking solutions through new areas of resolve.

I think a lot of fighters struggle with those what ifs.

"What if" this and "what if" that, and even a guy like me, who sees facts as they are, without a need to complicate them with emotion, had a few.

"What if the UFC hadn't taken the deal off the table back when I left Bellator?"

"What if I had fought in the UFC through my peak years?"

"What if I got out of the way of that flying knee Jorge hit me with?"

"What if my hips weren't shot?"

In the end, you can never know, and for that reason it's a fruitless exercise to bother with them for too long.

It sucks to not win. It sucks that I didn't get what I wanted, but it boiled down to this: there was no way I could train for another three or four fights to keep up the pursuit. Knowing that, I made up my mind to call it a career. My first order of business was announcing it.

Or rather, how to announce it.

I didn't want to call the UFC and let them know my decision before announcing it publicly, because, honestly, I didn't want them to talk me out of it. I had heard the rumors about some plans they had for me going forward. I was a huge draw for them in 2019, and the fight with Maia was awarded "Fight of the Night" honors, earning me an extra $50,000.[81] I knew from having conversations with the UFC brass and from people around that they'd have loved to roll me out a few more times, that the incentives would be in play to get as much out of me as they could. It was in their best interest to keep me going.

Part of me wanted to. This is where fighters sometimes get stuck, especially earlier in their careers. There's this attitude to never give up, to be tough, to keep grinding, to work through adversity, and that mindset is super beneficial to being successful. It's an intricate part of what's going to get you to the top. But you see it all the time when fighters get older—so many just hang on too long. There comes a time that you have to be honest with yourself and to be clear. You have to reassess and say, this is what my goal was, this worked or didn't work, and now I'm done.

I was done.

As I flew back over the Pacific, I decided what to do. I'd already been on Ariel's show seven or eight times that year, as he had the most bandwidth to get the message out there. I'd go on with him for his Monday show the following week to make the announcement, and that's what I did. After I'd explained my decision, I called the UFC and thanked them for giving me the opportunity. It was a genuine moment, and it was a sad thing to have to do. I'd been undefeated for almost a decade. I had plans to do so much more. I got to chase the dream I wanted to chase, which is all I could've asked.

I shot Dana a text thanking him for the opportunity, too. He fired back a dozen words, which was one of the longer conversations I'd ever had with him. "Pleasure," he wrote. "Thanks for the awesome promotion of the fights you were in."

Fucking Dana.

---

81   Oh, how far I'd come since all those accusations of being a boring fighter!

Talent doesn't exist.

If I want to piss people off, I'll just say that talent doesn't exist, just to be ambiguous. You can take a philosophical statement like that a whole bunch of different ways and approach it from plenty of angles. But I think there are inherent differences in all of us, whether it's height, size, speed, genetics, predispositions, personalities, whatever.

But talent itself doesn't exist.

Hard work and training aren't talent. Talent, as we know it, is just a word that helps us get past the minutia of the details. It's a convenient designation that implies something innate rather than something earned.

Take an example like the hundred-yard dash, which is a pretty simple event. You just run straight forward as fast as you can until you cross the finish line. Researchers will tell you that training can make a 19 percent difference, which might sound negligible on the surface. But do you realize the difference between a 10-second hundred-yard dash and an 11.9-second hundred-yard dash? They're not in the same universe. At a high-level event, a difference of nearly two seconds is an eternity. World-class athletes aren't talented. They are workers.

With the kids I'm around at my wrestling schools, I hear some people saying things like, "That seven-year-old is so athletic," as if he or she was born that way. Well, what have his parents been doing with that kid for their seven years on Earth? Have they been telling them to sit on the couch and watch TV, or have they been outside actively roughhousing with them? The difference you make with a kid between the ages of zero and seven is immense. Have they been coddled and told to be careful their whole lives? Or are they used to tumbling through the air? What is their relationship with gravity, with correcting their momentum and balance when they are knocked off-center?

I believe in proprioception. It means to understand where you are in space. It means to feel comfortable while spinning through the air. My kids will get that better than some, because I'm always throwing them around, holding them upside down, wrestling with them, pushing them. They are on a constant spin cycle, to the point that it's second nature to them, versus some kids who've never had that happen. Some might say my kids are talented or that they're athletic. No, they've had these experiences and are comfortable with their bodies being flung around. Any younger brother in a household is probably tougher than a boy who's been in a household where at the slightest hint of danger someone says, "Be careful!"

What we think of as "talent" is taught, and what we see as "athleticism" is learned. If we can manipulate one aspect of behavior, why can't we manipulate others?

One of the great examples I like to give within the realms of wrestling and fighting is aggressiveness. Is aggressiveness beneficial to you? Of course it is. It's 100 percent beneficial in wrestling and fighting. Yet it's something that's bred into us or out of us. By the age of two, every kid in the daycare has been told to "stop hitting" the other two-year-olds. "Don't do that!" they are warned time and again, with the expectation that they'll understand. So what happens? By age four there aren't any kids just going up and punching other kids at the daycare. Why? Because they've been taught at age two not to be aggressive. So we can see that that specific behavioral characteristic can be manipulated by the environment at two years old.

Why are we willing to admit that aggressiveness can be manipulated at age two, but we're not willing to admit that dealing with adversity can? Or that work ethic can? Or resiliency? Or all these other things? If you're willing to admit that being aggressive can be manipulated at a very young age—

and it obviously can—why aren't we willing to admit that those others can, too? Why the limitations?

These are the logical things I think about, especially when dealing with competition. Good work ethic can be taught. Dealing well with adversity can be learned. We only have to be willing to admit as much as parents, as students, as coaches, as athletes.

I like to think of myself as proof, as the living example of what I mean.

I talk to my wrestling kids about it all the time.

In fact, I'll walk them into a trap—I'll say, you've seen this happen, where kids are told not to hit other kids? They say, yes, of course. Then I say, if that can be taught, what about work ethic? What about keeping an open mind? What about dealing with adversity? Are those innate? Are they native instincts from birth? Or are they taught? My point of the argument is to illustrate that they're indeed taught, introduced, and harnessed. Just as passivity is taught and embraced, because how many six-year-olds just go to school and beat people's asses? None. (Or very few.)

It extends to other areas and occupations, to places like writing, for instance. It doesn't start with just picking up a pen and writing words. Maybe a kid has parents—or an uncle or grandparents—who wrote or read all the time that gave them a grounding that the intake and outtake of the written word matters. Maybe it was a teacher who made it click for them, with positive feedback. It grows out of that at a young age. The trick is to make kids fall in love with it as a pursuit. In wrestling, it's the same thing—turning it into something they enjoy.

The mental characteristics of competition are a big deal, especially when you're a kid, but I think about them even more as a dad. Are you going to bounce back from adversity? Can you? Do your parents coddle you, or do they tell you to get up and deal with it? Do you coddle your own kids, or do you let them work through the troubled times? Obviously there is a fine line here. You don't want to be *too* cold. You want to have a certain amount of empathy. But in any complex skill—which is pretty much everything in life, writing is a complex skill, fighting is a very complex skill, running a business is very complex, etcetera—dealing well with adversity is mandatory.

At one point with wrestling, I made a list of twenty-five skills, ranging from the mental to the physical. Will these twenty-five skills help you become a better wrestler? The answer is yes. I could take that part for granted. But which twenty-five? And what kind of score distinguishes how much better you become? Do they need to be 8 out of 10s? Nine out of 10s? Ten out of 10s? Do they need an average of 7.5? Where do you need them? And what ages mean what? Can you judge every one-year-old on that scale? By talent, we mean born with something. A lucky thing. A cosmic thing. Coming out of the womb is the only time you're talented or not.

But talent doesn't exist.

It is at odds with so many dogmas in the fight game to blow up such fantastic notions. We love the word "talent." So many people have to believe in their own talent to get where they are going, hang on to what they might see as destiny. They want to believe in hope, too. Hope is not for me. If I don't believe in talent, how can I believe in hope? People who thank God after a fight, or dedicate their victory to God, or lose and point to God's master plan—that's all fine, but I never found any of that too practical.

I don't really have a religion.

So I never wasted moments saying things like, "I'll leave it in God's hands." I try to make myself accountable for my successes and failures, to leave things in my *own* hands. Nor did I understand, in the strictest sense, people who say they are fighting for their kids. I would argue that people who say they fight to give their kids a better life are relatively misguided because fighting is a terrible profession. I always had to keep such things separate and honestly never felt a need to evolve my initial reasoning even when I became a dad.

I fought because I enjoy fighting. That was it.

Understanding the "prize" side of it is fun from a business perspective when you become a professional, but it never stops being sport. I want to win. For me. For my hard work. I want to be the best. There is a business component in fighting in MMA, but with wrestling all those years before that, I did it for free. I did it because I wanted to be good at it.

And I loved it. With my whole being, I still love it.

I always asked myself—and if I figured this out I'd be a billionaire—what made me, from a young age in the sixth and seventh grades, so driven to succeed? The best I can come up with is that I wanted to work. I wanted to get better. I wanted to be good. All this is true.

But what *exactly* was it that gave me that?

I struggle with that question. It's something I simply can't answer, even though it happened for me. My parents were supportive in the right ways, and I had some good coaches—particularly in high school—but a lot of people have that situation. None of that's totally unique. I had good support, but what was the fire that was driving me to be good? The thing that ultimately drove me to compete at the highest levels, to win awards and titles in the sports I competed in, to make the Olympics come hell or high water? Was it because my dad brought home some wrestling mats? That I'm on the spectrum? That I was picked on as a chubby kid? That my football team in the fifth grade didn't want to compete, which activated a switch?

If I could tell you what that was, and I could give that to other people, I would be a very rich man. The truth is, I don't know. What I do know is that it wasn't talent. I made the most of what I had, and I gave it everything I had. Through that I experienced heaven and hell for myself, and persevered. That's the whole truth.

CHAPTER NINE:
Psychology

"In life, particularly in public life, psychology is more powerful than logic."

–Ludwig Quidde

Going back to my earliest thoughts of competing, I've had this fascination with sports psychology. That's one of the reasons I was drawn to Muhammad Ali as a kid, because he saw the game at a certain elevation above the playing field. He was in a class of his own when it came to the mental side of competition, and that spoke to me right away. I liked figuring out specifically what made me tick because, in the meta sense, I was my own best experiment. I could make my actions bend to my will, and I could make my will just as stubborn as I wanted.

As time went on, I began paying attention to what made other competitors tick, too—teammates, opponents, coaches, haters on online forums, anyone. Going back to that first Fargo tournament I entered as a teenager, I learned how to strip away nonessential thought patterns and distractions to get into an optimal competitive mindset. I learned quickly not to blow situations up bigger than they needed to be, to ground myself for each competition with a kind of perpetual even keel. I always wanted my pulse to be exactly the same.

I also learned not to be in awe of my fellow competitors at that first big tourney. It's pretty simple; if the goal is to beat them, awe isn't helpful. All I needed to know was that I'd put in the work. I was ready. I wasn't going to get outworked. As time went on I knew I'd been there a thousand times. A million. Those repetitions muted the tensions and circumstances. Each time out my mindset was the same, to the point that it was as if competition was just an extension of normal life. As a competitor, I trusted everything would work out because of what I harnessed so dedicatedly on the mental side.

Psychology is a major component in sports. It's an even bigger function of combat sports, where the competition is one-on-one and weaknesses aren't so easily concealed.

When I was still competing at Mizzou, not long after I'd won my first national title, there was a student who hung around the wrestling room named Renee Mapes. She needed to spend two hundred hours with a team in order to get her PhD in sports psychology, and—as luck would have it—she chose the wrestling team to study. I was naturally drawn to her work. We started having conversations about a competitor's mindset—preparation and preparedness, repetition, work ethic, the right approach versus the wrong approach, how to retain what is valuable, and better yet, how to stay in a constant state of learning.

I can't remember exactly whose idea it was, but, with a mutual affinity toward the subject, at some point we decided to pair up for a book about sports psychology—her because she was en route to becoming an actual sports psychologist, and me because I was a known athlete with an aptitude for it and proven results. As part of our research we sent out a questionnaire to every NCAA wrestling champion over the last fifty years, spanning 1956 to 2006.

We asked basic questions that gave occasion for each champion to detail their mindset. "What was the biggest mental obstacle that you had to overcome in order become a champion? In your opinion, what characteristics made you an NCAA champion that other people did not have? Was wrestling a year-round quest? What was your mindset towards practice? What was your mental mindset towards competition?"

The answers contained common threads about hard work and dedication, but somewhere within them a magic picture began to come into focus, which helped define the "competitive drive." The most notable question we asked was a two-parter: "At what point did you become a great wrestler? What made you become a *great* wrestler as opposed to a good one?"

The responses to these were totally fascinating.

It was almost unilaterally, "I was *never* great."

This was worded in many different ways, and qualified through many perspectives, but it was the gist of most of the answers.

I was never great.

Given that these are media-savvy athletes, we'd antici-pated a fair amount of drowsy clichés to come back—"I got a new coach and that helped me turn the corner" or "I got new training partners" type of responses. Our hopes were to catch a few outliers who might take the time to enlighten. For the overwhelming response to be *I was never great* was somewhat astounding, as well as telling.

All those previous generations of champions—these indi-viduals who achieved so much in the sport of wrestling, on whom history reflects so well—didn't see themselves as great. They never bought into the hype of their achievements. We saw humility in the responses. We saw deflection or qualifi-cation. We saw things like, "Oh, if we're talking greatness, Dan Gable was great, but I just happened to be really good this particular year..." or "Your question assumes that I was great, well, that never happened, *but*..." Then they'd answer the ques-tion best they could after that qualifier. These answers, even in retrospect, were striving, even if they were telling us they'd never achieved what it was they were striving for. It dawned on me that championships were nothing more than a byproduct of what they were after.

The book was never finished.

We got off track, and we just couldn't align as the years went on.[82] Thinking back on it, though, some of the chapters we wrote ended up being pretty good. We had a chapter in there that I still apply when coaching my kids at the academy and believe in 1,000 percent called "The Beginner's Mind." It's basically a Socratic approach to competition and attitude.

Having a beginner's mind means you don't know everything and you want to learn more. It's about not being too proud to listen or too good to care—basically remaining open to new information, even as you begin to succeed. You might not necessarily know where the source of information comes from, but remaining open-minded is a key to that athletic success. Information can derive from unique places. It can come from a coach who never wrestled or a guy you beat. Just because somebody's not as good as you doesn't mean they have nothing to offer. That's so important, to trust that there is valuable information all around and that there's always room to grow. The way you think about yourself matters, and keeping the ego separate from the results is a must.

A classic example is this kid I coached at camp a couple of times named Yianni Diakomihalis, who later won three NCAA titles at Cornell (and was working on a fourth at the time of this publication). I helped him out when he was twelve years old, and I remember he was *always* asking questions. With Yianni it was "What about this position?" or "What do you think about this?" It was never "Well, this is the way I do it, and it works so that's it." He'd ask for clarification on this, better methods for that. He wasn't afraid to try things even if what he'd been doing worked. He wasn't wrapped up in superstitions. At twelve years old he was ingesting as much information as he could and trying to truly absorb all he was being taught. To him, asking questions wasn't a waste of time; wasting time was *not* trying

---

82   A couple of years later we revisited it and revised things a bit, but then she got busy and started her own practice. Perhaps now that I've taken the time to write a sports memoir, the next step is to finish that sports psychology book.

to get everything he could from the sessions he was devoting to the wrestling mats. He was there to learn and to get better. When he began winning national titles in college, he was still asking questions.

He'll never stop asking questions or trying to learn.

His success comes from that beginner's mind Renee and I were talking about in the book.

I always try to model that with my kids when coaching, too. We do a lot of sparring, and—before, during, and after— we'll ask questions. I will usually offer up something along the lines of "Well, this is what I think about it, but that's not the final answer," which simply means "This is my opinion, but that doesn't mean we're not hearing your opinions also." The desire to learn is the desire to get better. It's also an opportunity to view and review everything for yourself until you start to understand what it'll take to make you the best at what you're doing.

Not to get all self-helpish, but looking back at all those champions who answered the questionnaire, I find the fascinating thing is that for most of them, greatness was forever in the offing. When I reflected for a moment on that in college, it occurred to me that I didn't think of myself in those terms, either. Even after winning an NCAA title and the Hodge, I didn't use a scale of "Am I average, good, or great?" My focus was always on "Okay, how do I get better? How do I beat this guy? Is my single-leg good enough?"

Being as good as you can is in the action-forward specific. Greatness is in the abstract.

This was a key revelation.

Or maybe it was an affirmation of something I'd subconsciously understood for a long time. Greatness is never *really* attainable. It can't be. To stay hungry means to never become content, to never stop learning. Mentally the mind is in pursuit of that abstract greatness that can't easily be defined, but the one—and perhaps *only*—controllable approach is to just get better very pointedly, to zero in on a problem and fix it, to pinpoint what can be strengthened and strengthen it. By degrees. By increments. By time devoted to your craft.

I didn't quite realize just *how* important all that was at twenty-one years old, but as I went on I knew it was everything. If you get to the level when you think, *I'm good enough and nobody can teach me anything*, you stop growing. You recede. Your motivation wanes. Your ideas dry up. You don't just pull over to enjoy the scenery, you become part of that scenery forever. People pass by you, and you lose the competitive edge.

This all occurred to me at a moment when so many were calling me one of the greatest folkstyle wrestlers in NCAA history. For a guy with a noticeable level of success in the wrestling world, still very much in his college prime and rewriting the record books, it humbled me to acknowledge that. I loved hearing it, but when I showed up to work I tuned it all out. From where I stood as a national champion, it guarded me against complacency, and I think it helped me return hungrier to do it again my senior year.

It's a big lesson when you're talking about ego to outcome.

The ego is complicated, especially when outside forces are basting it continuously by telling you how good you are. Some kids think, *If I lose this wrestling tournament, people will think less of me*. It's a harmful way to think, because the end result of that mindset is performance anxiety. When the ego is concerned with what a loss might say about you and how it will be perceived, you've essentially put yourself on eggshells before a competition. And some kids attach *far too much* importance on a given performance.

They think, *It's not only a wrestling match, this is who I am*, literally identifying with the outcome. That's really stupid.

The problem starts with tying the ego to the idea of "I am great" or "I'm the best." The outcome for that kind of mindset is regression, because that's the only direction you're affording yourself. By *not* thinking in those terms, the greatest collegiate wrestlers of all time got really good (as in, started winning national titles). It wasn't because they didn't have self-belief, but because they understood something profound about self-sabotage. For me, understanding my own sports psychology was imperative to success.

I can nerd out on these things for weeks on end, but I like to think that I got a little lucky, too. I had that growth mindset from my earliest memories of competing, rather than a fixed mindset. It might not have been totally innate, but it was my natural state of mind. I wanted to learn as much as I could from the earliest stages of competition. More specifically, I wanted to figure out the best approach to make the Olympics team, which was the major goal I set my focus on as a kid. It's good to have a goal that pushes you to the limits you'll need to go and ultimately requires your very best effort.

The longer the odds, the harder you work.

I alluded to this before, but, looking back, the thing I really believed in wasn't that I was better than anyone, or the best—it was that I would improve. In fact, the very first thing that I ever believed in, genuinely, was that I'd be better than everyone *eventually*. I believed beyond a shadow of a doubt that I worked harder than everyone else and that hard work would pay off. What an advantage that was. To realize that if you're better than me this year I'll be better than you next year. I *believed* in progress. Especially the speed of my own versus others. You beat me by ten points this year, I'll beat you by two the next year. Leonardo da Vinci once said, "Poor is the pupil who does not surpass his master, poorer is the painting which does not excel the sketch," and you know what? That's pretty much how I saw it. With enough time, I would surpass everybody in my weight class.

When you believe in something like that—truly believe in your work ethic while maintaining an eagerness to improve— it gives you confidence, because it's something you put into motion to make the results follow suit. It's a mental and competitive advantage that remains in your control. The old "win or learn" adage gets kicked around a lot in combat sports, but it's true—when your default way of thinking is "the next time I'll do better," it serves as determination to do just that. Progress means forward, and "doing better next time" is a dangling carrot to snatch.

Mine was nothing more than a blue-collar progression with an eternal beginner's mindset. It paid off for me in wrestling. I didn't mind winning ugly; that's why I innovated my style to overtake the country's best in college. I didn't mind finding my own way. I positively loved knowing what I was capable of and going out there and showing it. I didn't like losing, but when I did it made me better. Between my high school class of 2002 and my college class of 2007, I was the most successful folkstyle wrestler in America. I think the mental side of it played a huge role.

In fact, I know it did.

When talking about psychology I have to say...it was always fun to get into my opponents' heads.

There was a wrestler at Oklahoma State named Brandon Mason, who, as a two-time all-American that finished in the top five, was relatively good. But he wasn't on my level, and he knew it. He would just play this really defensive style in our matches, not trying to win so much as survive. I always struggled to pin him, which, of course, was his entire objective—to nullify me just enough to lose with his head up.

One time during weigh-ins at the national duals my senior year, I was like, *Fuck this guy.* In college, when you weigh in you do it next to each other, yet he was standing behind Johny Hendricks, who was a weight class below us, to avoid any unnecessary eye contact or interaction. He wouldn't come anywhere near me the whole time. So after Johny weighed in and we got up there I saw my moment to take a shot.

I said, "Hey Brandon, are you going to wrestle me today, or are you going to run like a little bitch like you usually do?" That got to him. I remember he looked at me and didn't know what to say. He finally came back with, "I'm...I'm...I'm going to wrestle you," and he puffed up his chest.

I'd got to him.

So what happened in our match?

I pinned him in a minute. He did something stupid right off the bat because he was all fired up. That was exactly what I wanted to happen. It was a fairly big match, and I wanted to get him out of his comfort zone, out of his normal mindset. It was perfect example of walking somebody into a mistake they wouldn't normally make; by making him hyperaware that I was onto his sad mission to merely survive (with a not-so-subtle jab of calling him a "little bitch"), I got him to let his guard down. It was a mental trap to knock him off his moorings.

As impervious as I've always tried to be toward trash talk and letting people get into my head, that kind of thing can work. To be honest, I am always a little surprised when I can take somebody out of their competitive mindset and make them emotional about a fight. It runs so counter to every instinct to do that. Maybe it's partly because I'm on the spectrum, but somebody's not-nice words toward me never hurt or rattled me all that much. Then again, as a pragmatist, maybe it's partly because I long ago identified and accepted my own shortcomings.

One thing every fighter should be is realistic with themselves, not only in trying to identify your own weaknesses, but in embracing the idea that people will try to use those weaknesses against you. You can't be self-conscious or offended by those perceived weaknesses when they are brought to light. If I think I have the greatest physique and somebody calls me schlubby, more than likely my feelings are going to get hurt. If I think I can move with blinding speed and precision and somebody points out how *slow* I am, I will take that personally.

But what happens when you've already admitted that your physique is dad-like and your movements are barely faster than glacial? I identified pretty early on that I don't have an Adonis body and/or blazing speed, and because I teased *myself* about those things publicly it became hard for somebody else to pick on me about them. I owned it. By acknowledging exactly who I was up front, I made myself an elusive target before the first punch was ever thrown.

It goes back to self-awareness.

If you're honest with yourself and admit your own weaknesses, then it makes it difficult for people to embarrass or shame you. You've already acknowledged it! You're in on the joke.

Still, I messed with a lot of the guys mentally before fights because I figured out something that I still believe is generally true: fighters are so used to being feared, in their private and public lives, that to be treated any other way bothers them. A lot of people won't question a fighter of a certain standing. A fighter can create their own image, for the most part, and believe that inflated image is the true representation of who they are. These types are fooling themselves. The lack of self-awareness keeps them in a false place, which is easy to upset by simply not fearing them in the slightest.

Going back to Ronda Rousey, I think she created an image that wasn't true. She was being talked about as a world-champion boxer, and she embraced it.[83] When they talked about her being able to beat Floyd Mayweather and she rode along with it, there should have been an emergency intervention from those closest to her to make sure the fantasy elements of such a grandiose statement were considered just that: *fantasy.* Somebody should've pulled her aside and said, "Are you on fucking drugs?"

She wasn't a striker!

Because she was a great athlete who also happened to be super aggressive, people were worried about her takedowns.

---

83 She herself talked about it!

They were worried about the judo elements of her game that she adapted so well to MMA, not the striking. And as for that striking, the primary weapon of boxing? She was slightly above average, so any talk of boxing Mayweather (or anybody else) was 100 percent delusion.[84] Some fighters have a bubble built around their aura, and nobody is willing (or courageous enough) to tell them that it's bullshit. So, these fighters buy into it all. They run with it until they fall, and then they're stuck.

I knew my striking wasn't a strong suit. My wrestling was my trump card in just about every matchup I had. I didn't make any secret of this. There weren't any delusions in play. My plan was to hit you early on to get you to open up, get into a clinch, and then take you down and beat the living shit out of you. Some wrestlers develop into decent strikers based on a constant threat of the takedown.

Me? Nah. I'd rather plant a guy into the soft earth and keep them there. It worked through all my years competing, despite everyone knowing it was coming. I was as transparent as you can be as a fighter, and I never had a round where I didn't take somebody down.[85] I knew that if I could clear the initial gap without taking too much damage, I could just keep trying over and over (and over) again until they broke. If some media hyperbolist had looked at my brand of dominance and told me I could compete with Canelo Álvarez in a boxing ring, I'd have been the first to laugh in their face.

Not that some opponents, through the course of the prefight hype phase, didn't try to psych themselves up to believe they could prevent me mauling them on the ground. They talked themselves into believing they could somehow thwart or alter things by training takedown defense. I would just remind them

---

84 I think part of the delusion in Rousey's case came from her fight with Bethe Correia, whom she knocked out in Brazil. Because she scored a knockout rather than a quick submission, which everyone was expecting, hyperbole went roaring into the red.

85 Actually, with Jay Hieron, there had been a round or two where I couldn't take him down, and I was forced to stand with him. I think I won one of those rounds on my feet, so either my striking was better than people thought or Jay's was far worse.

that what was to going to happen was altogether inevita-ble.[86] And it was, for the most part. Even in my fight with Jorge Masvidal, if he doesn't catch me off guard with a flying knee, I believe I'd have walked right through the entire alphabet of whatever game plans he'd came up with—Plans A, B, and C.

Speaking of Jorge and in keeping with psychology, the one thing that fans like to point out about that fight is that I'd *angered* him beforehand—that I'd pissed him off to the point that he had no choice but to go out there and kick my ass. He *did* knock me out, which probably felt like comeuppance to some for having such a shrug-off attitude about him as a fighter, but come on! I actually executed my strategy well in the lead-up. Psychologically, just like with Mason in college, I wanted Jorge to fight emotionally. People were like, "*Oooh*, now you've done it—now you've made him mad!" Well, that's what I wanted! It didn't work out, but he was in the state I wanted him in, because nobody fights well if they're mad.

I used the same tactic in wrestling all the time. If I could annoy the shit out of somebody I was competing against, I'd do it in a heartbeat, because they're not going to perform at their optimal best if they come in there an emotional mess. Contrary to what people believe, a fuming mad competitor with murder in his eyes doesn't make for a more dangerous competitor.

It usually makes for a fool carrying around an unnecessary mental burden.

One thing I've noticed throughout my years wrestling, and especially in my later years in professional MMA, is that people in combat sports have thin skins—the fighters, the promoters, the trainers, the media. There are a lot of feelings in play at all times, and I am not a feelings guy. I think I fit in brilliantly because I was immune to getting my feelings hurt, yet I was

---

86 A dogged wrestler, if he fails once, fails twice, fails three times, oftentimes he'll at some point say, "Okay, the approach isn't working, I'm not going to take him down. I'll try to do something else, maybe try to knock him out." For me, I was always stubborn. I just didn't give up easily. I kept trying to take you down even if I met with extreme resistance early. See, the thing is, I can't not do what I am equipped to do.

perfectly willing to trample some feelings if I could. It amused me to see people get triggered so easily. Why did people get so worked up? Feelings are such fleeting things, and they aren't all that hard to redirect.

In other sports they talk about "bulletin board" material. You know, where somebody says something that pisses the other team off and gives them extra motivation to go out there and curb stomp the disrespectful party. They talk about this like there's an extra level of incentive waiting to be tapped by otherwise perfectly respectful competitors.

But to believe in bulletin board material is highly stupid. You're telling me there's another gear that can only be accessed when angry?

If you want to be the best competitor possible, you're going to remain as consistent as you can in terms of preparation and attitude every single time out, without variation. The even keel I talked about earlier. It's not that you want to be the very best version of yourself; it's that there *should only be one version*—and that version is always at its best. There is no such thing as a bonus level that can be tapped by the right insults. The notion that you'd need somebody to say something to get you more fired up to do your job right—whether we're talking football, baseball, darts, whatever—is...how can I put this politely... super *fucking dumb*.

If the kids in my wrestling room have to hear someone say something bad about them to get them fired up, then I'm not doing my job. They should be working harder on a much more regular basis, not because somebody said hurtful things, but because they are striving to be the best. I want them to work hard because they're in control of their drive.

Now, if we're talking after the fight or the match? It might feel a little better to have beaten somebody who was talking shit.

I think back to that fight I had with Karl Amoussou. After I put a beating on him it felt a little better because I didn't really like him. Usually, I remain ambivalent toward my opponents, and once the fight is done it's done, but he rubbed me the wrong way with all his banter beforehand. I admit, my smile was a little wider after that one. Then again, in my fights with top-flight guys like Douglas Lima, Andrey Koreshkov, and Shinya Aoki, I had no beef with them whatsoever. In fact, I kind of liked those guys, which made me feel a little guilty for what I did to them.[87] But just because I liked them didn't mean I wanted to do my job worse.

Take Robbie Lawler. I didn't say anything to him in the lead-up to our fight, not because we're friends or anything, but because I appreciated him, and I got the sense that he was okay with me. He was an old-school guy, a former champion who'd been doing it a long, long time. I had a lot of respect for him, and I felt he had respect for me too, which was nice, considering "respect" was a major subplot for that first fight in the UFC.

Did he punch me in the face less hard because of that? Hell no. He tried to take my fucking head off. He would do that whether or not I was talking shit.

I've been accused of giving my opponents bulletin board material since the original fan forums in high school, when I trolled all those pathetic adults and walked around pissing people off with my boom box. ESPN even used those very words during the NCAA Finals when I was taking on Keith Gavin, saying that I was particularly unconcerned about the match. I had said, "I don't plan on being stopped; I don't plan on being beaten. If that challenges my opponents, good, I want their best," and that felt like bulletin board material.

Was I being dismissive? For sure! But only because I didn't feel I could be beat. I was just being honest. Honesty can seem offensive to people who are deluding themselves.[88]

The psychological aspect of fighting plays into so many other areas, too. "Respect" is a buzzword in the industry, but

---

87 Just a little.
88 My honesty pisses a lot of people off, actually. It can seem rude and disarming when I say something honest during small talk at a social function. What can I do? Subtlety isn't my strong suit, and I've never learned the art of sugarcoating my messages to people.

having respect shouldn't rock you off your foundation or make you forget who you are. Over-respecting an opponent is a fairly common thing in MMA, given that so many fighters build names over time (like Lawler and Maia). Healthy respect is one thing, but that's nothing more than a nod to what they've accomplished or who they are.

Respect can be conflicted, too. It can be complicated—contradictory. You might respect a guy's work ethic but still think he's a asshole. There are a lot of those in MMA. You can respect his toughness, or you can respect his intelligence or the fact that he brings the best out of you. You can often tell when you have the respect of your opponent, too, even if you're unsuccessful against them.

Somebody like Chris Pendleton. I developed a lot of respect for Chris over the years. I went against him eight times in college and was only able to beat him once, and I think he respected the fact that I dealt with that adversity and that I refused to give up. I respected his ability to create new game plans for each and every match to keep me off guard. I can remember thinking, this is how he beat me last time, so I'll approach him this way this time. It was like playing a game of chess with him, only he remained a step ahead. I respected his intelligence, his ability to evolve, and the fact that he competed so well against a guy he'd already beat. That's harder than some might think. Sometimes when there's a rivalry, if the loser doesn't give up and keeps coming back stronger, the winner starts feeling pressure. There can be a tendency to get lulled into an "I've already beat this guy, and I have nothing to gain anymore" thing, which is a form of complacency. Yet he knew I was gunning for him, and he understood I was always narrowing the gap. He was forced to step things up to remain ahead, and—kudos to him— he did that.

The same could be said for my rivalries with Jake Herbert and Keith Gavin, yet I was on the opposite side of the ledger in those. I went 5–0 against Jake, who won the 2009 Hodge, and I was 4–0 against Gavin. Keith actually came at me each and every time we went at it. He didn't play the defensive game that others do, just trying to save face. He was a tough, aggressive competitor who was giving me his best every time; therefore, I had to match that intensity and give it my own.

I've always viewed trash talk as a natural component to prize fighting, a necessary evil in the profession, because you're literally selling a fight to the public. For me it is never personal, which worked as an advantage against those for whom it was. Yet occasionally there are fighters who take things a little too far. Colby Covington is the prime example of somebody who crosses the line of decency, which I wouldn't have a problem with if only he were sincere in what he's saying.[89]

It's nice to get a person off-center, but in fights like Conor McGregor's lightweight title bout with Khabib Nurmagomedov, even an emotionally rubber guy like me squirms just a little bit. Conor is great about getting into people's heads. He did it with Dustin Poirier in their first fight back at UFC 178, to the point that it felt almost unfair. He did it to José Aldo, too. There are a whole bunch of guys who fought really stupid fights because of McGregor's ability to get into people's heads, especially earlier in his career before they'd identified his tactics. In that way, much like Muhammad Ali, he's been fairly masterful at not only building big fights, but also in gaining the mental edge.

With that Khabib fight, he went all in. I mean *all in*. He brought Khabib's family into it, as well as his manager Ali Abdelaziz (whom he called a terrorist), his religion, everything. He did this after trying to throw a hand truck through the window of a bus Khabib was in months earlier in Brooklyn, which helped make their eventual fight into the biggest UFC

---

89 So much of it is tired shtick, which takes away the sting a little bit—rule number one is it's better to be authentic than a bumbling try-hard.

pay-per-view of all time. Did Conor go too far with the trash talk in that case? It was somewhere I certainly wouldn't have gone, but if that's how Conor believes he's most effective, then he has to do what works for him.

It ultimately *didn't* work against Khabib, though, who showed up and did what Khabib does well. He trucked McGregor with the same cold blood he trucked everyone else he faced. People use the word "stoical" when talking about him, but I just see a guy who is never less than dialed in to the task at hand. Khabib may have some hatred for McGregor, but he didn't let that affect his performance. Afterward, after he tapped McGregor out and the mini-melee that kicked up, when he launched over the fence and tried to talon-swipe some idiot with bleached hair? Only then did he let emotion play a role. If Khabib ever smiled, he'd have smiled a little wider after that one.

The thing is, trash talking can be an art form.

Growing up, my family kind of gave each other a lot of shit, which made me a natural at it. It thickened my skin a bit, too, waging all that verbal warfare with Max. And spending five years on the Mizzou wrestling team—where everything was crass, crude, and ribald—prepared me for just about anything.

I've always enjoyed it.

Talking shit publicly, with all the reporters eating out of the palm of your hands and printing your every word, just enhances the whole effect. It's not for everyone, even those pathetic few who don't realize it.

It's definitely an area where somebody like Colby struggles. Colby tries to be a shit-talker, but he has lines that he delivers with a kind of oblivious jocular buffoonery. He's not smart enough to go off script from the lines he's rehearsed in the mirror a thousand times, so he forces them even when the occasion is all wrong. You have to read the room a little bit and improvise to be good at it. If Conor starts in and feels something, he runs with it. His ability to read the room is phenomenal.

In fact, Conor's greatest moment in my opinion came after that fight with Eddie Alvarez at Madison Square Garden, right after he won the second title and was the apple of the fight game's eye. He said, beginning in the most humbling tones, "I've spent a lot of time, Joe, slaying everybody in the company. I've ridiculed everyone on the roster. I just want to say from the bottom of my heart, I'd like to take this time to apologize...*to absolutely nobody*. The double champ *does what the fuck he wants.*"

It was such a great line. So in the moment. So *perfect* for the moment.

He felt it. And he nailed it. Using the microphone well, whether it's shit-talking or setting up the next move, is also an art form.

I still kick myself for screwing up my hot-mic moment after the Lawler fight, when I barked out "Is that the best you got?" in hopes of fucking with Dana White. Given that the fight was so chaotic and I took damage and narrowly pulled it out, and that it was slightly controversial, it didn't exactly fit the situation. Had I gone out there and taken Lawler down and submitted him no problem, it would have been a great line. But I should have deviated. I got caught up and I didn't improvise well in the moment, and shit like that bothers me. Bad execution. I got caught up and fixated on something I wanted to say.[90]

Regrets, as they say, have stayed in business a long time—even for those who don't believe in them.

But I love the psychology of competition the way I love the feeling of breaking a guy within that competition. It's the game within the game, getting them out of their ideal state of mind and into a state of discombobulation. It makes me think back to Tyrone Lewis, whom I wrestled many times, notably at the US Open Finals and in the Olympic Trials Finals in 2008.

Tyrone was an intimidating guy, which made him generally successful because he was actively out there trying to

---

90   I wasn't as bad as Colby, though, because that would be impossible!

intimidate people. The way the governing body FILA did it at the time was really dumb; you had to take two of three periods to win. I knew I had him shook at the end of the first period because he was grumbling and amping up the pummeling aspects. In wrestling, you're allowed a certain amount of pummeling, and I could tell Tyrone was coming undone.

At that moment I saw the chink in the armor, and I thought, *Oh, fuck yeah.* So I hit him as hard as I could right back, and the ref stopped the match to warn us to knock it off with a couple of seconds left in the first period. As the referee stopped us, Tyrone said, "Let's take this to the parking lot." Right there in the heat of a wrestling meet I said, as calm as you please, "Hold on, I got one more period to beat you here and then we can take this anywhere you want to." He didn't like that. You could literally see it dawn on him that that intimidation factor didn't work. His go-to tactic in this case was a Hail Mary, and it was extremely ineffective.

That bummed him out. He was used to being feared.

Sometimes the mental play can translate a little better, especially for strikers in MMA. A fight can be finished with a single big shot, which is an advantage for somebody trying to force his opponent into one false move. I can't finish a fight with a takedown. For a wrestler it's got to be a progression. I can get somebody to throw a bad punch so that a takedown is easier, but then I have to actually do the work after that. There are steps involved leading to a finish.

If Conor gets José Aldo to come in swinging in a manner he wouldn't normally, and Conor puts him away with one well-timed left hand, it's curtains for Aldo. The mental side of that forced the error that led to the business end of Conor's knuckles. In fighting, things are skewed to benefit the striker more so than the wrestler. In wrestling, at a high level, if you were to get a five-point move, chances that you win the match are relatively high, so you want to get your opponent into a mistake. In MMA, if you get somebody temporarily fighting like an idiot, flash knockouts are a thing.

Looking back on my career, especially from the vantage point of being a coach for the kids at my academy, there are things that become clearer to me at a remove. As a competitor, you're dialed in to beating the guy in front of you. You're into winning state tournaments, regional tournaments, making the Olympics. You can identify what it is that makes you tick and see the results in real time, along with your improvements.

It's a different perspective being a coach. Things are more vicarious.

It's tough, because you only get to see the kids a handful of hours a week, while they're with their parents all the time. There are some kids who will never get over the hump because their parents have planted bad ideas and philosophies into their heads, things they're now carrying around as second nature. When you meet a kid at age ten, they are super young, yes, but they've had ten years of whatever their parents' philosophy is ingrained in them. I see it more now than ever: the opposite of a growth mindset is a fixed mindset, where whether you're good or not, the ego's always on the line. If you lose, you suck. If you win, you have it figured out.

Some kids have a solid foundation at home but just need to get over the mental hump. I had a kid a couple of years back who was fast becoming one of the best in country in his weight class, yet he had trouble with tying his ego to stuff. He was amazing at the local level, where he could show up and win simply because he was that much better than everyone else within that limited pool. He was praised for it and basked in the attention.

Yet, when he would get to these national tournaments, there were problems. He needed to perform optimally to beat these guys, who were the best of the best, and he wasn't doing it because he had a mindset that if he lost people would think less of him. Either that or he'd build a tower of his opponent and lose faith in his chances, thinking, *Oh, I can't beat him.*

I knew the truth was that he could.

He had a fail at a national tournament that fall, and that spring he had a legitimate shot of making the 17U world team, but he got into his own head and wrestled poorly, finishing fifth. At worst, given his ability, we thought he should have come in second. So we had a very pivotal sit-down talk with him after that tournament, telling him how he was holding himself back from reaching his full potential. It wasn't unlike my first national tournament in Fargo, when I was caught in awe of the talent around me and my coach for Team Wisconsin, Terry Steiner, gave me the same kind of talk. I told him that he's holding himself back and reminded him that he's as good as these guys. You could see it click. I recognized it because I remember when it clicked with me.

After that talk he went on this streak where he won the Junior Duals, beating a couple of highly ranked guys, then he turned around and won the Junior Nationals. Then he took off. After that he was ranked No. 1 in the country in his class. His name: Keegan O'Toole. He's been No. 1 in the country pretty much ever since, and won a national title at Mizzou as a freshman. You can change those things in kids, but they've got to be open.

And in other situations, the parents have got to be open, too. Especially when you get kids at a younger age, when you can infect them with the way we, as coaches, think, and if the older kids buy in they get the younger kids to buy in, as well. The young kids always look up to the older kids.

I see these things as a coach. I lived them as a kid.

The best of the best have that beginner's mind and remain open-minded, and they can understand where they're failing with the idea of fixing those things. In a fixed mindset, when things don't work they always blame something else. It's the coaches. It's the environment. It's that they're just not strong or fast enough. It's *other* and *outside*, things beyond their control. The fixed mindset will always center on a thing to blame, or an excuse, rather than looking internally and addressing the central question: *Where do I struggle*? That one little question gets to the root of the problem, and, in answering it, champions are made.

People ask me all the time about my most cherished achievements, what means the most to me out of the things I've accomplished. I always say that winning that first state title was affirmation that I'd dedicated my life and passion to the right thing. Winning my first NCAA title was sweet, too, and I was beyond thrilled to fulfill my promise to Coach Brian Smith at Mizzou. Winning the Hodge and making the Olympic team are relatively equivalent, and two of the proudest accomplishments of my life. I remember they did a ranking going back to 1995 of the Top Twenty-Five Hodge seasons, and I think I took the No. 3 and No. 6 spots. From a folkstyle wrestling perspective, I can compare with anybody who's ever competed. Not too many people can say that and mean it.

But really, the moments that involved my teammates having success were equally as joyful over the years. When Mark Ellis won a national title at Mizzou, that was a tremendous thrill for me. He was my roommate for four years, and I saw how intensely focused he was through that time, as well as all the obstacles he had to overcome. When my brother Max won a national title, I've never felt happier for someone in my life. I knew how hard he'd been striving toward it for so long, and to be with him as he broke through was something I'll never forget. When my teammate Tyron Woodley went on to win a UFC title, I felt it as deeply as I'd felt any of my own personal triumphs. These were momentous moments in my life, and there's a kind of bond that I shared with those guys that is almost too personal to convey effectively here. Those guys had worked a long, long time to achieve what they did, and I'd been there to see the hard work the whole way. I'd sweated with them. We'd suffered together endlessly yet pushed each other through. To finally see that kind of hard work pay off for them, that's one hell of a feeling. And remember: I'm not a feelings guy.

People ask me, too, where I'd rank myself in the pantheon of great welterweights to ever compete in MMA. It's a tricky question because I don't really think in those terms, and, of course, I am slightly biased even though I am an unapologetic realist. I like to believe that if I'm healthy and in my prime, I can compete with a Matt Hughes, a GSP, a Tyron Woodley. I like to think I'd have fared very well against Marty Usman, and that if Khabib wanted to try his hand at 170 pounds he'd have been in for a long night.

I know at my very best, I can hang with any of them.

I've never publicly made the argument about any of that, because the simple fact is I didn't do it when I had the opportunity. There were reasons I can throw out there. My hip being what it was when I finally came to the UFC being chief among them. The UFC pulling the deal off the table in my prime. On and on. But I know what excuses sound like (and how they read when written in a book). I can look objectively at the facts.

Given the circumstances, I didn't do nearly as much as GSP or Tyron in the end. Had I been given similar opportunities to compete against the best guys when I myself was at my best? Who knows. This question can't resolve itself, so it forever lives in speculation. I can only look at what happened and be thankful that I had the run I did.

Those guys deserve the credit.

Even Jorge Masvidal deserves more credit than is given him, and, in fact, far more credit that I've afforded him in this book. I get annoyed when people say, "Masvidal could never do that again," meaning that what he did was a fluke. Maybe. But the fact is, he did it once. Once on record is all it takes. That's all he needed to do. I can't change it. How many times did he need to do it for people to give him full credit? The fact of the matter is it happened. It's over.

I can live happily with what I've been able to do, and I can feel, once and for all, contented in what I accomplished. I have little artifacts I can look at to remind me of the journey. I have wrestling trophies and MMA titles, which I keep in a box somewhere. I have images of a cocky, wild-haired kid getting his hand raised, smiling ear to ear. I have people who helped me, those who pushed me, those who forced me to work harder and to make my earliest dreams into a reality— my coaches, my teammates, my friends. I have this crazy memory, which replays the most minute sequences of every match and fight whenever I want to think about them. I have kids at my gym who want to learn from me, and a family who loves me. I have my kids; my wife, Amy; my brother Max; my parents, who got me that wrestling mat when I was a kid and just wanted to roughhouse.

I gave my heart and soul to wrestling, and wrestling gave me everything I ever needed. I brought the wrestling to MMA, and I dared anyone to show me there's a better foundation. I fought the fights I needed to inside and outside the world of combat sports.

I won, I lost, I competed.

If the ten-year-old me who dropped all that weight to take wrestling seriously could fast-forward to the end of this story and see all that was to happen, I know he would pump his fist. Just as I can look back at that same ten-year-old kid and be proud of just how determined that little bastard was.

EPILOGUE:
OH RIGHT, THAT LITTLE BUSINESS WITH JAKE PAUL

The fight game is a funny thing.

Just when you think you're done, somebody comes along and disturbs the peace. In this case it happened to be Jake Paul, a YouTube personality I'd never heard of before watching the highlights of his fight with former NBA guard Nate Robinson in a celebrity boxing match in November 2020. As I've done a million times, I randomly made a comment about the fight on Twitter. Everybody was making comments about it on Twitter. Yet, somehow, he saw my tweet, and it must have struck a nerve because he began calling me out.

Right away my competitive antennae went up. My first thoughts were, *Who the hell is this douche? And when did that brand of jocular buffoonery become a thing?* But I could see how popular he was and that he was drawing a lot of attention to himself in the fight world, so I couldn't ignore it. A fight with a moonlighting internet guy? That would be fun!

I'd just had my hip replacement surgery on September 1, which kept me hobbling around for a few weeks on crutches. By late November, less than three months removed from going under the knife, I was feeling damn good. The chronic pain had subsided for the most part, I had a broad range of mobility that felt liberating, and the healing process was right on track. My doctor told me it would be a full year before I'd be completely healed, but I didn't think I needed that long.

I'd been watching John Wayne Parr, a kickboxing champion who'd had the same surgery as me. He was full go after just three months, and I saw him out there kicking shit just as hard as ever. With the prospect of an unexpected and highly lucrative fight opportunity at my door, I hit him up and asked him just how the hell he was doing what he was doing, and whether or not what he was doing was wise. He gave me enough encouragement that I felt compelled to call my doctor to find out why I had to wait so long if he was out there so soon after his own hip replacement. The doctor gave me some medical speak about healing properly and mentioned that Parr's surgeon had a higher rate of failure than his own. I asked him what his personal rate of failure was, and he said it was 1 in 998. One in 998? That's a needle in a haystack.

I said, "Fuck it, I'll take my chances."

By December, three months after my surgery, I was working out regularly again. I eased into it at first, overly cautious not to aggravate anything. I definitely had some doubts. It was one of those things where you think, *Hey, I hope my new fake hip is with me a really long time and I don't have to get it redone.* But that slowly went away. I was riding the bike fluidly, lifting weights, sparring lightly, just getting back into the swing of things. I felt good enough that in January, after some public back and forth between our camps, I committed to a boxing match with Jake Paul. I wasn't "coming back" or anything. It was just a one-off bonus bout that I couldn't refuse.

The official announcement of the fight was met with no small amount of curiosity from the fight world. Most saw it as something between a money grab and a lark. Obviously, Jake's desire to fight me was strategic. I was a retired MMA champion and a decorated wrestler, which to the Jake Paul generation translated as somebody formidable in combat sports. But I wasn't a boxer, and Jake knew that. The media knew that. I fucking knew that. The most scrutinized aspect of my entire MMA career was directed toward my striking ability, or lack thereof. I was a potential notch for Jake.

This context is what made the fight enthralling for a random novelty attraction. Jake was 2–0 as a professional boxer, with a victory over a fellow YouTuber and a guy whose biggest claim to fame was winning an NBA dunk contest. I was 0–0 as a boxer, but I had decades of competition under my belt. Would my general big-fight experience trump some fight-game inter-loper's flight of fancy? That was the selling point. To use pro wrestling parlance, it was the one time in my life where I was the babyface in a matchup, with Jake being the heel. People wanted me to shut his ass up.

Some were even wondering if I'd just say screw it and take him down, ignoring the rules of engagement just to have a little fun. It was a fight that piqued people's curiosity in the wildest ways.

Once it was signed, a few doubts came fluttering in. I was a little worried that I'd discover I couldn't train the right way and I'd have to do the unthinkable—pull out of a fight with a blowhard YouTube guy. That idea was in the back of my mind as I began training, but I pressed on and didn't encounter any setbacks. In fact, I felt a ton better than I had the last few years of fighting in MMA. I was thirty-five years old, but I felt better than I had at any point in my thirties.

The most frequent question I got for taking the fight was, "Why?"

Contrary to the popular narrative in the media, it wasn't a money grab—though that was certainly part of it. I stood to make a nice bag of cash for an arbitrary not-really-out-of-retirement fight that was closer to an exhibition than a professional bout. But the simple answer is that I just love to compete. It's not something that goes away after you hang it up, even when you're satisfied with what you've been able to achieve. Having a date circled on the calendar is an exhilaration that I can never get enough of. As I've tried to explain in these pages, I'm not afraid of failing, either.

I brought this story up recently to a high school senior I coach who is way better than anybody else in his weight class and fresh out of challenges. I was talking to him about potentially helping his team by moving around weight classes. To me, that idea was tantalizing. When I was in high school, our wrestling team wasn't that good, but during my senior year, when I was leaps and bounds ahead of anybody in the 171-pound weight class in which I competed, my coach allowed me to move wherever I wanted to. There was this one kid who was ranked No. 1 in a smaller division who kept talking all this shit to me, not knowing I could go down to 160 to settle it.

I showed up at this big midseason tournament at 160 and smashed his ass. That was gratifying. Later that year, at the conference finals, there wasn't anybody there to challenge me at 171 pounds, so—even though I weighed in at 166 pounds—I wrestled up at 189. I took on the guys who took second and fourth in the state, each outweighing me by nearly 25 pounds, and killed them both. That, too, was gratifying.

I felt confident that I would do exactly what I did in each case, but there wasn't any guarantee there that I would succeed. That unknown was exhilarating in its own way, the possibility—or maybe even the expectation—that I could fail.

A lot of my own kids these days don't have that attitude. They think, *Oh, but he's bigger.* Back then I didn't give a shit; I just wanted to compete. Old habits die hard, I guess, because when Jake came calling I still didn't give a shit, even if the risk of failing against a guy like that outweighed whatever rewards were in play.

It was an experience, to say the least. I got to go out to Los Angeles and train with the great Freddie Roach, the storied boxing trainer who has worked with everyone from Manny Pacquiao to Julio César Chávez. I'd have never had that experience if Jake hadn't come calling.[91] Freddie put me in there with this one really good boxer, a world champ named Gabriel Rosado, who thoroughly whopped my ass. I mean, he was cracking me hard, which had me protesting! I literally had to stop the round and tell him, "Listen, I'm not good. I know I'm not good. You need to chill out over there, because I'm not trying to get knocked out in practice. If I get knocked out in sparring I can't go make money. If I go get knocked out by Jake Paul, at least by that point it's over. I made my money. If I get knocked out by you, it's all for nothing."

He eased up after that. But I knew my limitations against a seasoned boxer. Was Jake seasoned? No, but I didn't know exactly how good he was based on the little information I had on him. The fight was being promoted by an upstart company called Triller, which turned the thing into a kind of circus atmosphere on fight night in Atlanta, with drunk commentators, celebrity locker room shit-stirrers like comedian Pete Davidson, and various musical acts such as Snoop Dogg, Ice Cube, Justin Bieber, and the Black Keys. I was like a square dad being dropped into a party in Ibiza, with Oscar De La Hoya slurring his words as he called the action.

It was strange. People didn't know what to make of the whole thing. Dana White's distaste for me is nothing next to his distaste toward Jake Paul, the latter of whom was poking at Dana on social media all the way through the fight. White said he'd bet Jake a million dollars that I'd beat him, which

---

91 Roach was cool, and I think he gave me clarity on some things. I did an Insta-gram Live when I was getting set to leave Los Angeles about this, but he shows up at his gym and gets guys to the highest level. That's who he is. I coach wrestling, but I've never coached wrestling exclusively. Freddie made me realize how much I want to coach wrestling full time. He was inspirational. Watching somebody who loves what he does and is that good at it was great.

Jake ran with publicly for the next couple of years.[92] I'd been in the business of making Dana money for a short time, but this wasn't one of those nights. I knew I wasn't that good, and I was sensible to my own level heading in. This was my first boxing match.

My take heading in was that Jake wasn't likely all that good, meaning I only had to be a little better. I'd only been knocked out by Jorge in twenty-plus years of competition, and, even in using the four-ounce gloves, I'd never really been rocked in my other MMA fights.[93] I figured that even if he was better than me I could weather the storm and grind him out a little bit, because he'd never really been in a real fight before whereas I had been in many. Once he got tired I could take it to him, as there was no way I'd fatigue first. I knew I could push, and I wanted to know if he could.

Unfortunately for me, Jake was significantly better than we thought he was going to be. I hit him with a pretty solid punch early on, which somebody snapped a great picture of, and I was a little surprised that he ate it as well as he did. I was hoping he'd go down when that connected. A centimeter to the left or right, who knows, maybe he would've. But he didn't. He only hit me a couple of times, but the right hand that dropped me landed flush. I've never gone back and watched the fight, but, of course, the KO went viral. The aftermath was brutal, as I had to hear it from fans for months. But my immediate thought was, *Oh well*. Amy was there with me, and she said, "What is your life right now? Justin Bieber just opened up for you?" I said, "Let's go get my check," and we started laughing.

I didn't know if Jake was any good at boxing before the fight, and I didn't know if he was any good after that fight. I just knew I wasn't all that good. It wasn't until he fought my friend Tyron Woodley in his next bout that I realized he was

---

92   As far as I know, Dana never paid.

93   Except maybe in that fight with Lyman Good, though it was an upkick he hit me with, and I recovered pretty quickly.

better than people were giving him credit for. Tyron would've easily beaten me in a boxing match, and Jake beat Tyron not once but twice. Jake takes it seriously, and I have to give him his props.

Was it a dumb idea to come back for that last little ladle of humiliation? Hell no. It was kind of like the wrestling days during my senior year; you think he can beat me, let's do it. I wasn't scared to jump into an unknown situation to see how it might play out. I didn't have my ego tied to the outcome. The whole experience was fun up until I fucking lost. That part sucked.

As for diminishing my legacy, I honestly think that a lot of people are tapping into their own emotions and feelings about how embarrassed they would be in that situation and trying to put those on me. Obviously, it's annoying to lose to Jake fucking Paul, but when I signed up for the fight, that was a possibility. It was just something stupid. Somebody asked me if I wanted to fight, and I said, "Sure, sounds like fun, let's fight." It was never, "I want to cash in one last time!"

I'd be lying if I said the money wasn't a lure. I made close to a million dollars in less than two minutes. That's roughly what I made during 2019 in three fights with the UFC as one of its biggest attractions. That's around the same amount I made during my last year competing with ONE Championship, and it's far more than I made in all of my Bellator fights combined, which totaled around $340,000 through nine total fights and four title defenses.

Yeah, I cashed a nice check.

But money wasn't the reason. I did it because that's who I am. If I was exposed by taking one last chance, so be it. I can proudly say I've never known another way.

ABOUT THE AUTHOR

Ben Askren was one of the most iconic collegiate wrestlers in NCAA history, amassing a record of 153–8 at the University of Missouri, taking home two national titles and twice winning the Dan Hodge Trophy for being the best college wrestler in the country. He represented the United States in freestyle wrestling at the 2008 Olympics in Beijing and later used his wrestling pedigree to win titles in two separate promotions once he transitioned to mixed martial arts. When he retired in 2019 at the age of thirty-five, Askren was not only one of the most accomplished fighters in combat sports history—he was also one of the most popular. He currently hosts the *FloWrestling Radio Live* podcast, as well as the *Funky Crypto* show. He coaches at his wrestling club, Askren Wrestling Academy (AWA), which he owns with his brother Max and his high school coach John Mesenbrink. They operate five locations in Wisconsin. Ben lives in Delafield with his wife, Amy, and children Alex, Andi, and Ozi.